SERVICE IS MY BUSINESS

Printed in United States of America

Service

Is My

Business

High ethical standards in business and professions; the recognition of the worthiness of all useful occupations; and the dignifying by each Rotarian of his occupation as an opportunity to serve society.

—FROM THE OBJECT OF ROTARY

ROTARY INTERNATIONAL
EVANSTON   *ZURICH*

"But you were always a good man of business, Jacob," faltered Scrooge, who now began to apply this to himself.

"Business!" cried the Ghost, wringing its hands again. "Mankind was my business; charity, mercy, forbearance, and benevolence were, all, my business. The dealings of my trade were but a drop of water in the comprehensive ocean of my business!"

—CHARLES DICKENS, *A Christmas Carol*

Dedication

VOCATIONAL service is something that no one else—no leader, speaker or committee—can do for you. It expresses the prime function of your club as proclaimed in The Object of Rotary.

"To encourage and foster the ideal of service as the basis of all worthy enterprise . . ."

That means in particular your "enterprise"—your daily work—the business or profession described in the classification you represent in your Rotary club. The privilege of holding this classification entails the obligation—"to put Rotary to work where you work"—to make *service* rather than self the basis of every principle, policy and procedure in your job.

It is a large order.

Many find it difficult. Some avoid its personal application by lip service to generalities. Others are frustrated by not knowing where to start.

Service is My Business is an attempt to surmount these obstacles by conveying the meaning of vocational service in terms of actual experiences. Reading about them, you should become more keenly aware of the opportunities that lie close to hand.

To those Rotarians whose efforts have provided the substance in these pages, this little book is respectfully dedicated, and if the situations described do not always reflect your particular problems you are urged to bring your own flame to these fagots, to seek in your own enterprise or calling the specific challenges to make service *your* business.

NOTE: As a member of the Aims and Objects Committee for 1946-47, Past President Percy Hodgson saw the need of making vocational service more realistic for the individual Rotarian. This idea was seconded warmly by the late James Watchurst who was on the committee the following year. The enthusiasm of these two business men resulted in the first publication of *Service Is My Business.*

CONTENTS

THE OBJECT OF ROTARY

✳ ✳ ✳

To encourage and foster the ideal of service as a basis of worthy enterprise and, in particular, to encourage and foster:

First. The development of acquaintance as an opportunity for service;

Second. High ethical standards in business and professions; the recognition of the worthiness of all useful occupations; and the dignifying by each Rotarian of his occupation as an opportunity to serve society;

Third. The application of the ideal of service by every Rotarian to his personal, business, and community life;

Fourth. The advancement of international understanding, good will, and peace through a world fellowship of business and professional men united in the ideal of service.

1

A Clarion Call

AN incident in one of Molière's gay comedies involves a letter which a "shopkeeper turned Gentleman" plans to drop at the feet of a lady of quality. Seeking help in writing it from a rather pompous teacher, the shopkeeper insists that the letter should be written in neither verse nor prose.

"It must be in either one or the other," the teacher tells him.

"And when we speak, what is that then?"

"Prose."

"Upon my word," the surprised shopkeeper exclaims, "I have been speaking prose these forty years without being aware of it."

SERVICE IS MY BUSINESS

Can it be that Rotarians who protest that they do not understand vocational service share the bewilderment of this shopkeeper? How often the complaint is heard. Vague, intangible, theoretical, are a few of the many criticisms heaped upon this phase of the Rotary program. Yet of all things, vocational service is the most simple and practical—the *prose* of each man's life and occupation.

Prose can be dull—dull as the daily grind of earning a living over days and months and years of servitude. Or prose can leap with inspiration and sparkle with fun as does the life of any business or professional man or humble craftsman who has discovered the opportunity for service in his occupation. Servitude or service? That is the choice of everyone everyday as he takes off his coat to go to work. How he views his occupation is all important. The view depends upon the point of view.

The point of view that *Service Is My Business* is the simplest explanation of vocational service. All we have to do is to ask ourselves, and we shall understand clearly what it means. In my profession, for instance, *is* service my business? When it comes to considering the needs of my clients or patients or pupils, are their best interests in the forefront of my thoughts all the time, or am I concerned mostly with advancing my own career? When competition gets rough, and the other fellow is crowding me? When a strike threatens or an employee makes what would appear to be an unreasonable complaint? Or when a complaint of my own that seemed so thoroughly justified is airily dismissed? Is *service* my business? Is service *my* business when I

12

confront the hard decisions arising from changing prices, new processes, or new investments?

Service is my business—the explanation is simple enough. But the situations that business and professional men encounter in their daily work are vastly complicated. The climate for service may be harsh and discouraging.

An enthusiastic exponent of vocational service tells of his disappointment:

"The business in which I am interested is reduced to one-third of what it was six years ago and is still losing money because my competitors can undersell. Why can they undersell?

"(1) By underpaying the legitimate wage laid down by the wage agreement;

"(2) By working employees at cut piecework rates and making them take work home to be made up by their families;

"(3) By forcing employees to sign a receipt for the correct wages and actually paying half—even a quarter of that amount.

"My choice is either to continue to lose money, to leave the industry, or to join the unscrupulous manufacturers in their nefarious practices."

Disregarding the extreme circumstances of this Rotarian's dilemma, it places in sharp focus the difficulty that vocational service presents to many Rotarians and many Rotary clubs. Surely the solution of his dilemma is obvious. Yet it seems to have escaped him. Obviously, he must strive to amend "the nefarious practices" and to establish decent conditions for production and distribution throughout his whole industry. If he could accomplish that, how much the scope of his service would be extended, and yet it would still be *his* business.

The province of vocational service is misunderstood when it is limited to the aims and practices of Rotarians. The field is much wider, much more inviting to tangible and specific action, much less a delicate matter of the private conscience.

Vocational service is SHARING with others who are not Rotarians—SHARING with them the ideal of Rotary.

This concept of vocational service derives from the principle which is the very core of Rotary—the selection of members on the basis of classification. As a trustee of his classification, each Rotarian is obligated to share with others who are not Rotarians—and particularly with those others associated with him in business or profession—the realization that "service is my business."

Does not this view of vocational service as sharing remove every embarrassment and obstacle to activity? No longer is it a delicate matter of investigating the moral character of fellow members or complacent reference to their business or professional standing in the community. The course of each Rotarian is plainly marked. It is his job to communicate the ideal of Rotary —to explain its application to others in all the relationships of his business or profession—and to help others to embody it in their daily decisions and practices.

So conceived, vocational service is capable of demonstrations as tangible as the provision of comforts for the aged or the rehabilitation of a crippled child. And the duties of the vocational service committee are equally forthright. Members are to be shown practical ways of sharing the ideal of service in their business or profession. Their actual experiences are to be discussed and their efforts co-ordinated in projects sponsored by the club. The examples in the following pages should suggest to any Rotarian or any vocational service committee all sorts of possibilities.

"Vocational service is the challenge of Rotary," is the clarion call of one Rotarian. "It is the main feature which distinguishes Rotary as a unique organization among many societies the world over. It is hardly an exaggeration to say that it constitutes Rotary's main justification for existence in a world that needs the Rotary conception of service in vocation today as never before.

"For this is a time of change, a time when as never before in our lifetime, we have the opportunity in the midst of uncertainty to create a world in which conflict and class war shall give place to friendship and co-operation, a world which shall satisfy and not frustrate the toiling millions, a world based on the mutual recognition of the Rotary concept of service as the basis of all worthy enterprise.

"These things can be; we, fellow-Rotarians, have it in our hands, now, today and tomorrow, to work consciously for this nobler world. We can, if we care enough and dare enough. Surely we shall not fail our day and generation. Inspired and sustained by our common ideal we shall march forward together, pioneers, adventurers in an enterprise that will call forth our courage, our determination, and all our capacity for clear and constructive thinking."

No less challenging than the broad, social implications of vocational service are the results of individual self-examination. Dissecting the meaning of service in his business, the director of a museum in Switzerland sees it as a "plus," over and beyond the responsibility that he owes to the society which provides his livelihood. "I can undertake this responsibility lightly, sit through the appointed hours as do the proverbial bureaucrats. Or I can fulfill my responsibility scrupulously—do my work faithfully and take care of my personal interests besides. Thereby I can give exactly as much as I take and no more.

"I can, however, understand this responsibility in a higher sense, and start from the desire to see my work contribute to society. If I succeed in that, then I perform *service* and give the public back more than it gives me. In practice that would mean, in my vocation, that I develop and broaden the use of the museum through constructive thinking. I share the view of many of my colleagues that the museum can and should develop a much greater usefulness in educational and civic ways. If that is so and were it achieved, it would be just that 'plus' which I identify with service. Service is always thought for the future, the conviction that a better society can be created, a contribution to the future and belief in the future."

Men who have not lost their vision in spite of setbacks and disappointments—men who have built their business or professional lives around the aim of helpfulness to others and to the community of men—these find a sure reward. A Rotarian physician, invited to explain what service meant in his craft, described the humble laboratory that stands near the Victoria Memorial in Calcutta, India. It was here that Colonel Ross discovered the cause and method of the transmission of malaria. A modest plaque carries this legend in verse, written by Colonel Ross himself:

> This day relenting God
> Hath placed within my hand
> A wondrous thing, and God
> Be praised, at his command
> Seeking His secret deeds
> With tears and toiling breath,
> I find thy cunning seeds,
> O million-murdering death.
> I know this little thing
> A myriad men will save:
> O death, where is thy sting
> Thy victory, O grave?

The physician continued: "How great an honor was given Ross that millions who never knew his name should breathe and know life because of him? And what shall I say more, for the time would fail me to tell of Caler and Deaver and Murphy and the Mayos and Koch and Roentgen and all the host of others who through ceaseless vigil and an irresistible desire to know the truth subdued diseases, obtained cures for pernicious anemia, stopped the ravages of diabetes, quenched the violence of tuberculosis, out of weakness were made strong, waxed valiant in fight, and put to flight the armies of sickness."

Each classification in Rotary could recite a similar rollcall of unsparing contributors, men who overcame many disappointments, risking criticism and material loss to raise the standards of their chosen vocation. There is not a man in Rotary who, looking backward, would not select as his most rewarding experiences the opportunities he has found to serve society.

How these opportunities develop out of the rough clay of daily business and professional practice, we shall now attempt to illustrate.

*In what ways does
your club help each
member to share
Rotary with
non-Rotarians in
his business or
profession?*

2

Dignifying an Occupation

Paul Harris, the founder of Rotary, was a lawyer. Jealous for the honor of his profession, he took an active part in the work of legal associations—local, state, national, and international. In those days of 1905, there was the gulf of a long tradition between members of the learned professions and those engaged in trade. Paul Harris felt deeply a need to bridge that gulf—to rescue the professional man from an isolation that was alternately lonesome and irritating—to dignify the occupation of tradesman with a zeal for its honor.

So to the first meeting in Chicago of the first Rotary club he invited a coal dealer, a tailor, and a mining engineer.

Men of different vocations, trades, and professions formed the first Rotary club. Vocation was the principle of selection at the beginning, and has remained the distinguishing core of Rotary ever since.

Let it not be thought, however, that the implications of this principle have remained unchanged through the years. The impact of practical experience on earnest men such as Arthur Frederick Sheldon stimulated a continuing development. An early member of the Rotary club, Sheldon established a school of salesmanship based on the idea that successful salesmanship depends on rendering service and that no transaction is justified unless both parties benefit. He gave to Rotary the slogan, "he profits most who serves best."

Nowhere is there more substantial testimony to the evolving character of vocational service than in the official phrasings of this avenue of Rotary. It appeared first in the constitution of the Rotary Club of Chicago (January, 1906). The first of the two objects reads as follows:

The promotion of the business interests of its members.

Before this aim is condemned as utterly selfish, the comment of a past president of Rotary International may be recalled: "Vocational service really started in the early clubs when they had an official known as a statistician whose duty it was to compile each week all the orders that had been given or received by members. But that kind of vocational service, we found, would not work. I am not ashamed of it, however, because *they were helping each other even then.*"

In 1912, this statement of vocational service was abandoned, and the International Association of Rotary Clubs adopted for the guidance of clubs and the individual Rotarian as the first of five objects:

DIGNIFYING AN OCCUPATION

1. *To promote the recognition of the worthiness of all legitimate occupations, and to dignify each member's occupation as affording him an opportunity to serve society; to encourage high standards in business and professions; to increase the efficiency of each member by the exchange of ideas and business methods.*

"The ideal of service as the basis of all worthy enterprise" was introduced in 1918 together with a rearrangement in order of the objects. In 1922, the paragraph which called for an exchange of ideas and business methods was dropped, and the word "useful" replaced "legitimate" in the first paragraph of the object as last quoted.

No further change was made until 1935, when the Six Objects were restated as Four Objects, and vocational service was presented in the phrasing that was retained in 1951 when it became the second of four avenues in the single Object of Rotary:

2. *High ethical standards in business and professions; the recognition of the worthiness of all useful occupations; and the dignifying by each Rotarian of his occupation as an opportunity to serve society.*

So the dominant impulse of vocational service, present at the start, developed and expanded. Helpfulness to others—not only to fellow Rotarians but to all the "others" who make up human society. Respect for others—not only the rather ambiguous "legitimate occupations" but all "useful" ones. Thoughtfulness of others—not only in the cause of increased efficiency— though that is important—but in every way that will extend the usefulness and consequent dignity of his occupation.

The dignity of a profession derives from the reputation of its practitioners for dedicating their learning and skill to the service of others rather than to personal profit. "In fixing fees," declares the American Bar Association, "it should not be forgotten that the profession of law is a branch of the administration of justice and not a mere money-getting trade." Doctors of medicine subscribe to the statement that "a profession has for its prime object the service it can render humanity; reward of financial gain should be a subordinate consideration." In so far as a business man earnestly applies to his working life the dignifying concept of "service above self," he too can aspire to professional status.

"I thank God that I am in the paper business," a manufacturer told a Rotarian clergyman. "I believe that it is a service calling just as much as your ministry. Everytime I see children carrying home bread and meat from the store wrapped in clean paper, I give thanks that I am permitted to serve them in this manner."

On the other hand, it should be apparent that the human relations that concern vocational service are just as challenging to the professional man. He, too, is obligated as a trustee of his classification, to exemplify and share the ideal of service with his patients, clients or pupils, with suppliers of his practical needs, and with colleagues or competitors. Even if he has few or no employees himself, he is still in a position to help people become better and happier employees. In association with Rotarians who are businessmen, he may be reminded how the dignity of his occupation derives from service.

"It has been said that in this town," reported a Rotary club in the Eastern Hemisphere, "certain members of the medical profession have not been living up to their Hippocratic Oath, and that in the course of healing they also clean out their patients' pockets. Washing of dirty linen among Rotary members may well have a salutary effect. It is proposed to arrange a symposium of a doctor, patient and onlooker to discuss the comprehensive picture, the difficulties, problems and prospects."

These critics were trying to defend the dignity of an occupation by providing an opportunity for practitioners to explain its contributions to the common welfare. Without such opportunities for defense, the rascality of a tiny minority of doctors with money-mania is used to justify general charges of clandestine fee-splitting, prescription of unnecessary treatments or surgery and the abuse of insurance plans. Miracle drugs and vaccines are given the credit for keeping people well while the old-fashioned doctor—sitting beside the bedside waiting for nature to take its course—is mourned. Opportunity to examine such charges before his Rotary club will be welcomed by any physician just as the representatives of education, law and religion rejoice in defending the honor of their occupations against similar accusations.

If these *professions* whose reputations for service are long established need to defend themselves, how much more is *business* subject to suspicion and attack. The target is so broad and so vulnerable at many points.

A cultivated distrust of business, in fact, is often one of the most formidable obstacles in the path of service, and Rotary clubs occupy a strategic position in helping to overcome it.

Can—or should—business aspire to the status of a profession? The question produces constant and fruitful debate. Present trends lend urgency to the quest for an answer. Even though profit is still the accepted prize in the great game of business, how the game is played, rather than the amount of the prize, is increasingly the concern of businessmen. The growth of educational requirements for business employment and the accumulating body of technical knowledge in each field suggest comparison with the professions. And, perhaps most significant of all, membership in trade associations arouses in businessmen a feeling of common loyalty and responsibility for the dignity of their calling.

One difference, however, does exist between business and the professions. By licensing the right to practice, the professions are shielded from the competition of unqualified individuals. In most business, by contrast, anyone possessing the minimum of cash or credit can get into the game.

Accordingly, the attitude that businessmen take toward their competitors is crucial to the success of their efforts in dignifying an occupation.

Who in your community
would you nominate to receive
a public award
for exemplifying
the ideal of service
in his or her daily work?

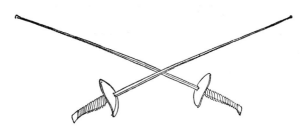

3

Dear Enemy

THE significant point in the following story is not that it concerns a late president of Rotary International who had many important interests and distinctions, but that it is the personal experience of one who had his business on the main street and who had a competitor. Let him tell the story in his own words:

"The thought came to me many years ago. I don't have to hate my competitor. There was a certain fellow I had been fighting with for years, and I thought of course he must be a chiseler. His only fault so far as I know was that he chose to make his living the same way I did, but at that, he seemed like a terrible fellow.

"Then a thought came to my mind. Somewhere in

Rotary somebody gave it to me. I called on him. We sat and had a chat. He turned out to be a rather decent sort of fellow. The first thing you know, we began to talk freely wherever we would meet. Then it happened that he had a great tragedy come into his life. One of his children was taken ill and died. He came over to me and said, 'I don't know how I want to do this thing. I wonder if you would come over and preach the funeral sermon for my little girl.'

"I was his enemy! He was my enemy! He was the fellow I thought I had to hate. We became very good friends. He still competes with me. He still gets all the business he can—but I like him just the same."

A rather similar transformation occurred in the central business district of a city in Chile, where trade was suffering from the bitter feuds of rival merchants. Under the influence of Rotary, some of these merchants decided to go more than half way. They called a meeting of all the business men in the district and got them to agree to a few very simple principles. As a result, the ruthless rivalry, the unfair practices, the defamations of character and products, ceased. Cooperation became the watchword even to the extent of joint advertising in the newspapers. The principles which they agreed to follow were very simple.

"Cultivate the friendship of men in the same business or profession;

"Beware that these friendly relations do not lead to price-fixing;

"Bar the imitation of brand names and the luring of employees from rival businesses;

DEAR ENEMY

"Do not ask in friendship what you would not ask in an impersonal business way;

"Forget the word 'competition' and use the words 'trade relation.'"

Whether the word "competition" is used or not, Rotarians generally would not wish to give up the invigorating effects of healthy business rivalry. Personal freedom and practical efficiency alike are fostered by competition. Business has to keep on its toes to survive. The customer has free choice where he will bestow his patronage. Better values, higher quality, lower prices court his approval. A multiplying range of choices is made available to win his favor.

The practical business or professional man will not shrink from a rivalry that does so much to improve service. Rather he will regard his competitors as fellow-players in a great game, mutually interested with him in keeping the rules and improving the play, just as necessary to his real success as his employees or his suppliers, or his customers.

Such would seem to be the attitude natural to a believer in the virtues of free enterprise. Yet how often a very different feeling prevails. The Negro, in his inimitable fashion, put his finger on it. His song, "Everybody Talking 'Bout Heaven, Ain't Gwine There," recalls that everyone talking about free enterprise does not necessarily believe in it. Some deep feeling of insecurity establishes barriers between competitors who could help each other and their community by their shared wisdom and enterprise. Grudges and suspicions develop that never receive honest examination. Or a certain embarrassment and wariness is felt in the presence of competitors, unspoken—unconscious, perhaps—but thwarting any real confidence. This last experience is so common, that the question often arises whether competition is really a blessing, or a curse.

Is competition a blessing or a curse? Rotarians who undertake their vocational service as a practical program for their daily business and not merely as an occasional gesture of self-sacrifice, should be quite clear in their own minds about the right answer to this question. Important consequences are sure to follow from the decision as to whether these craftsmen, in the same business or profession, are friendly allies in service—or inveterate enemies.

To argue that competition is a curse is to take a dim view of life itself, for in a sense all people are competitors. All sellers compete for the consumer's patronage. All buyers are in competition for the best products. That everyone is competing for his job with everyone else was illustrated by a vocational service program in which the competitor relations within a college faculty were discussed. "We need someone to keep us on our toes," declared a Rotarian editor. "That is where a fast-stepping competitor helps us. He makes us put forth that extra effort which wins. Should we hate a man who helps us to win?"

The Sherpa porter and the New Zealand bee-keeper who conquered Everest proved that life below can also be fine and the spirit of man magnaminous. Tempted by the little-minded to claim that he had reached the summit first, the Sherpa porter replied: "We went together. We were tied together. No man's single effort can put him on top of the world."

That competition is a blessing, on the other hand, is confirmed constantly in the growth of business communities. There is the classical instance of the department store in Chicago which sold adjacent lots to a competitor in order that a great shopping-center would arise to benefit both of them. The same idea motivated the Rotarians in Mississippi who helped to rescue a competitor from bankruptcy because they did not want to see an empty store on their main street. The Denver florists, likewise, who rushed equipment to help a rival whose greenhouses were destroyed by fire, were loyally sustaining a competitive relationship that had proved profitable.

If competitors help each other, consult about their business problems and methods, share their trade secrets for the benefit of the consumer, surely they are blessed by the knowledge that their business is being built on firm foundations. The nervous feeling that the other fellow has something up his sleeve diminishes. Energy is released for expansion.

Hydraulic brakes had been in use on a certain make of car for a year when it became known that another manufacturer planned to install them. The pioneer firm promptly phoned its rival to the effect: "We have had a year's experience and our brakes are just about perfected. Why don't you send your engineers over here and check what we've done before you go further with your plans?" How many lives have been saved through this sharing of a trade secret? Was it not good business, too, for *all* manufacturers using hydraulic brakes to make sure that they were built and installed according to the best experience available?

If competition is regarded as a curse, it is logical then to defame competitors, use "cut-throat" tactics to drive them out of business, and to seek to establish a monopoly. Such destructive tactics would be very short-sighted if competition is proved to be a blessing. Experience teaches that there is seldom a victor in a price war, even though it may be hard to persuade of that fact the customer who is lured by "bargains," "cut rates," and "economies." But even the customer may be convinced that the offer of something for nothing should always be viewed with suspicion. Some Peter somewhere is being robbed to pay Paul. It may be the sweated labor that produced the bargain in the first place. It may be the dealer who absorbs the loss. It may be the manufacturer who sees the hard-won value of his trademark debased.

Or it may be the customer himself who loses, through his other purchases outrageously over-priced —losing what he thought to gain from the "loss-leaders" that lured him into the store. As the realization dawns upon him that someone is being robbed, the customer loses his respect for business as a whole and for the price-cutter in particular.

On the other hand, agreements among competitors to allocate production and raise prices originate usually from the conviction that competiton is a curse. Evidence against the long-run profit of such restrictive arrangements is overwhelming. The Brookings Institution estimated that during the twelve year period between 1922 and 1934, the vast total of 248 billion dollars worth of goods could have been produced in the United States had it not been for these and similar restraints upon production. A loss comparable with the cost to the United States of the second world war is therefore traceable to the widespread conviction that competition is a curse. Yet think how many of the parties to these restrictive arrangements were ruined in the disastrous cycle of inflation and world depression that marked this earlier "post-war period."

Without exaggeration most of the dishonesties and weaknesses that afflict business in all lands are traceable to the open or secret conviction that competition is a curse. Because of it, great industries cower uneasily behind protections of many kinds, service is cramped by fear, craftsmanship by ca' canny.* What a wonderful opportunity for Rotarians in any and every community to open the windows and admit a bracing breeze of common sense and courage dispelling these miasmas that choke free enterprise, proclaiming that competition is *not a curse,* but a blessing; that their competitors are not insidious foes, but comrades in service.

If there is a prevailing feeling of cold suspicion, it is the first step that costs the most. "How much I hate that man," Charles Lamb once exclaimed. "Hate him?" asked his friend. "You don't even know him." "Of course I don't know him," Lamb answered. "If I knew him how could I hate him?" And so with competitors —what common-sense reason is there for hating or

---

*Original British labor slang: "A deliberate slackening in the rate of work or quantity produced."

fearing men who are grappling with the same problems, who share the same background and training, who have chosen the same job of social usefulness? How much can be gained by going more than halfway to win their friendship and co-operation.

Dear Enemy — perhaps the deepest reason of all for regarding competitors in this light is rooted in the very nature of life in all its forms. A farmer who had won many blue ribbons for the corn he grew, made a practice of sharing his best seed with his neighbors.

"How in the world can you afford to do this?" he was asked. "Your neighbors are entering corn in competition with yours at the fair each year. Yet you help them with your prize seed."

Said the blue-ribbon corn-grower, "Why, that's very simple. If I want to grow good corn I must help my neighbors to grow good corn, too. The wind picks up the pollen from the ripening corn and swirls it from field to field. If my neighbors grow inferior corn, the quality of my own will suffer. If I want to grow good corn, I must help them grow good corn, too."

The blue ribbons in all businesses and professions are won by those craftsmen who do not fear the bracing winds of competition.

What steps have you taken to
co-operate with your
competitors to improve your
common service to society?

4

The Modern Guild

IN ancient Damascus—the "pearl of the desert"—was the famed Street of the Swordmakers. Here, in one corner of the oldest inhabited city in the world, lived a guild of artificers, and here they produced the famous blades of Damascus.

These blades were so keen that you could cut a floating thread of silk with them; so elastic that they would bend almost double and then spring back as straight as ever.

Death—death by strangling—the most shameful punishment of the time—was the sentence passed on any member of the craft found guilty of producing an inferior product, because:

> He did place the proofmark of our most honored and trusted craft upon badly smithed and evily tempered blades which, having failed in the hand of the purchaser, brought great disrepute upon all the master swordmakers of Damascus.

It was as if each sword bore the fingerprints of its creator, a projection of his personality. And it is doubtful if these early craftsmen were entirely inspired by concern for the unlucky purchaser who might trust his life to a blade which had a defect that the eye of man could not detect. Rather they were motivated by a sense of indignation that their skill might be questioned.

When a Rotary club is formed, the first consideration is to secure as members, outstanding representatives of every worthy and recognized business and professional activity in the community. The same thought directs the selection of new members. They must be successful, that is, they must be skilled in their respective crafts. Their integrity must be above suspicion. They must be dedicated to the idea of supporting and improving the standards of their craft. Indeed, a Rotary club might well be described as an assembly of skilled craftsmen.

Unlike the ancient guilds, however, the Rotary club is not organized to safeguard and hoard the knowledge of particular skills. On the contrary, the Rotary club is dedicated to the task of extending the service which all skills can render to society.

The Rotary club, moreover, which selects its membership from *different* trades and professions contrasts

34

in that respect with the ancient guilds which associated men of the same craft. A closer comparison might be drawn with the modern trade-union except that the guild was built around employers rather than employees. It would seem that the nearest thing to a modern guild is the trade association whose membership largely comprises employers of the same business or craft, many of whom are direct competitors.

The absence of competitors in Rotary clubs in order to include a cross-section of all business and professional activities in the community entails certain obligations. One of these was expressed by the board of directors of Rotary International when it enjoined Rotarians that they "should not expect, and far less should they ask for, more consideration or advantages from fellow-Rotarians than the latter would give to any other business man with whom he has business relations." Any abuse of friendship for profit is foreign to the spirit of Rotary. In other words, free competition is a blessing that Rotary clubs are designed to foster.

Another and more positive obligation of the Rotarian is to carry the message and ideals of Rotary into his business relations with competitors. As a trustee of his classification each member is regarded as an ambassador to his craft and urged to participate actively in the work of his trade association. This obligation was stated very forcibly by the chairman of one vocational service committee addressing the members of his club:

> It is my duty as the spokesman for the vocational service committee, my fellow-Rotarians, to say to you in all earnestness and candor, that unless you are carrying

back to your craft, your trade association, or your professional group the ideals, the precepts, and the high standards embodied in Rotary, you should resign. You say that you are not inclined to bother about your competitor, that you are too busy with your own affairs to be concerned with what the other fellow is doing, that you are not inclined to take on the responsibilities of leadership in your line of business. I am sorry. The membership committee made a mistake when they let you in. Those who fail in their duty to properly represent their line of business or profession choke up one of the arteries through which the lifeblood of Rotary flows.

The Rotarian who is putting his shoulder to the wheel in his trade association derives many advantages. Not the least of these is goodwill. A striking demonstration of this advantage was given in the course of a radio program on vocational service, broadcast from one small-town station. The work of medical associations was cited as the reason why doctors are regarded almost automatically as valuable citizens. Because his association has established minimum standards of education, enforced codes of correct practice, provided for the exchange of new methods and discoveries, the individual doctor has a long start in earning a place of respect wherever he may locate.

The practical benefits that small business gains from membership were interestingly illustrated by a tailor called upon to explain the value of his trade association in a Rotary meeting. Looking back over a generation of business dealings in his town, he found that general wages had increased five times while the price of tailoring had only gone up three times. It was at the meetings of his trade association that he and his competitors had exchanged the "know-how" which had enabled them to increase the efficiency of custom-tailoring so that competition from "ready-to-wear" clothes could be met.

With the viewpoint of an outsider, an Australian Rotarian expressed his amazement on observing the discussions of a meat-packers' conference in Chicago. The domestic problems of individual plants were discussed before assembled competitors in a wholehearted and unreserved way. Besides raising the general level of the industry, these discussions proved that in a meeting of twenty men, any one individual stands to learn more from the other nineteen, than they in turn could learn from him. Yet in the commercial field, away from the conference, the Australian visitor found that these same men were engaged in the most vigorous competition which acted as a salutary stimulus to increased efficiency and the elimination of waste.

The advantage of belonging to the trade association being fairly obvious, it may be asked, what particularly is the Rotarian's contribution.

The indication that a larger proportion of Rotarians belong to their craft associations in towns under 12,000 than in the larger cities shows how much the small business man has to gain from the ideas and improvements in practice made current by the trade association. But what can the Rotarian himself, coming from a small town and operating a small business, contribute to the work of these large and impressive bodies?

A Canadian Rotarian responded to this question by recalling a childhood experience:

As a very small boy, I attended a rural school. There was one good-natured lad, not particularly clever, and with no particular gifts of leadership. The older boys were a tough and, in some ways, quite a vicious crowd. They used to tease this fellow unmercifully, but through it all, he preserved his good nature and steadfastly refused to deviate from his standards of conduct. The contrast of his good-humored determination had a tremendous influence. It's the same way in trade associations. Without the influence and exertions of sincere individuals, a cynical minority can accomplish much mischief.

The great statesman-author, Edmund Burke, once declared that "When bad men combine, the good must associate, else they will fall one by one, an unpitied sacrifice in a contemptible struggle." Rotarians combined can exercise a potent influence for good in their trade associations if they inject the larger vision of opportunity to serve society and the realization that only so far as the public is served can trade associations serve their own best interests.

That there is need for Rotary leaven in the practices of many trade associations was vigorously asserted during a discussion at one craft assembly at a convention of Rotary International. Too often it was charged, trade associations, instead of putting service ahead of profit, degenerate into pressure groups, conspiracies to circumvent government regulations, and merchandising corporations to control prices. Rotarians were urged to join forces against these tendencies and to support vigorously their association code.

An outstanding contribution of Rotary to the strength of the modern "guild" has been the development of codes of correct practices. In fact, it is generally recognized that the widespread movement by trade associations to adopt these voluntary commitments, sprang largely from the thought and effort of vocational service in Rotary. The results of this experience in drafting codes can be summarized briefly as follows:

(1) The code is not a law, but an expression of the determination of members in the association to maintain certain standards.

(2) These standards are stated positively and specifically as evolved from the experience of the particular business or profession.

(3) Example and friendly influence are the only ways by which the code is enforced.

The value of a code to a trade or profession depends largely on the fulfillment of these conditions. If it is limited to generalities, if it is out of date, if it is used only to adorn the wall or hidden away in files; it might as well or better not exist. The inspiration and labor which brought its adoption by the trade association may have been educational at the time when it was formulated, but now it no longer serves.

What finer opportunity for effective work in vocational service is offered than the methodical exploration of the status of codes?

Each member of a Rotary club might be asked to produce the code of his trade association for the purpose of critical comparison. In cases where no code exists or where the existing code consists of generalities or obsolete references, members may be persuaded to take action in their trade associations to repair the omission. In this great work, they should seek the wholehearted co-operation of Rotarians in their classification from other clubs who belong to the association. They can obtain much helpful guidance in these efforts from Rotary International.

Even those members of the club whose trade association can boast of an adequate code of correct practices have a task to perform. They can take steps to make sure that its standards are observed in their own business or professional practice, as a training manual for employees, by spreading its influence among customers and suppliers, and by references to it at meetings of the trade association to revive its authority among their competitors. Thus they may help to spur the development of a new sense of craftsmanship in these modern guilds. Thus they may repay the debt which, in the words of Bacon, each man owes to his profession.

How could your club
arrange for
a review by members
of their trade association codes?

5

Good Faith

THE codes of correct practices that trade associations adopt cannot be enforced by legal means. Often they concern details not readily covered by law, and pledge business to standards of conduct that make legislation unnecessary. Public opinion and the conscience of the individual who subscribes to the code are the only guarantee of its effectiveness. The success of codes depends ultimately on the good faith of individual business and professional men.

Buena fe como norma—habitual good faith—was the crisp interpretation given to the vocational service phase of the Object of Rotary by Rotarians of Latin America when they came to translate it into Spanish —just that and nothing more.

SERVICE IS MY BUSINESS

At first sight it might seem that a good deal of vocational service was ignored in this brief interpretation, but on closer examination it will appear that the core of meaning in the phrases—"high ethical standards," "recognition of the worthiness of all useful occupations," "dignifying by each Rotarian of his occupation" —has been preserved. Good faith between people is implicit in all of those statements, and also in the various relationships of service in business and profession. It is the essential ingredient of all transactions between buyers and sellers. When competitors can depend on each other's good faith, friendly co-operation follows as a natural course. Employers and employees will succeed in making the best of their jobs only when the integrity of each individual can be trusted and respected.

Buena fe como norma—invariable good faith—the core of vocational service.

Facing the aftermath of two world wars, the need for restoring good faith is evident. So much has happened to disillusion men and nations. Hitler himself broke eighty-seven treaties, and he was not alone. In resisting the invader and in the death struggle of nations, deceit became a weapon as lethal as the atomic bomb. A dark cloud of distrust seems to hover over the conference table whenever the peace of the world is discussed.

The restoration of good faith has become, accordingly, a primary concern of international organization. It is enshrined as the second principle of the United Nations Charter.

All Members, in order to ensure for them the rights and benefits resulting from membership, shall fulfill in good faith the obligations assumed by them in accordance with the present Charter.

The remedy—a promise to keep a promise—may not seem adequate, but at least it defines the need, no less urgent for individuals than for nations. The mutual good faith of business, so essential to prosperity and well-being, has likewise been sorely strained by the uncertainties and temptations of an unstable economy. How is it to be restored?

One way is to mark clearly the difference between good faith and good intentions. Members of a Rotary club in Japan were delighted when one of them announced that he planned to finance a tour abroad for two principals of local schools. He operates a chain of theaters, and he planned to contribute one yen for each admission paid during the course of a year.

While the plan was under discussion, however, it was learned that this man also operated a "strip show" in conjunction with his theaters. A friend protested to him that sending educators abroad for the betterment of future generations was a good intention, "but first you must show your good faith by closing down those places."

Torn between his better self and business profit, the showman at length agreed to convert those places into facilities for healthy amusement. "The march of the yen" began, and before long two principals were given a hearty send off by the Rotary club on their mission abroad.

No social system could exist without a general confidence that people will invariably do what they have contracted to do.

At the time of the great earthquake and fire in San Francisco, the plant of a large law-book publishing company was destroyed. All account books were lost. The indebtedness of lawyers to this firm amounted to thousands of dollars. The aggregate was known but there was no way of ascertaining individual amounts. To the credit of members of the American and Canadian Bar Associations, who practice law in accordance with the codes of those associations, it is a matter of record that within a few hundred dollars, the entire indebtedness was voluntarily acknowledged and paid.

Without confidence, no one would trust his employer to pay his wages and no work would be done without constant supervision. Trade would be reduced to barter with a club handy to reprove deceit. The enterprising business man would find no capitalist in whom to confide his plans and aspirations. Without the invisible sinews of good faith, society would disintegrate. Mankind would quickly relapse into barbarism.

To recognize that good faith is essential, however, carries no assurance that it cannot be destroyed. Just to assume that it is habitual with the vast majority of people, merely begs the question. How is habit created? What is the secret of this invisible tie that binds men to their tasks and to their contracts?

The answer is quite simple. People learn to do by doing, and by watching and emulating others. Good faith becomes habitual through a host of affirmative actions, and by the reverse process it can also be destroyed. The little things count. A single man doing his task patiently and faithfully strengthens the whole fabric.

Disraeli once said, "Next to knowing when to seize an opportunity, the most important thing in life is to know when to forego an advantage." Were Disraeli a contemporary, his remark might well have been inspired by the leader of a popular orchestra of considerable renown which gave a concert under the auspices of a Rotary club for the benefit of the club's student loan fund. At the time, informal arrangements were made for a similar concert to be held the following year.

Meanwhile, the orchestra was offered a more lucrative but conflicting engagement in the same town by another sponsor. Despite the absence of a signed contract with the Rotary club, the leader of the orchestra refused this offer without first obtaining the consent of the club, which was readily granted.

What an uplifting example this incident provides! A man's respect for the sacredness of his word matched by the unselfish "foregoing of an advantage." The story could end there and its point would be clear. But there is a sequel.

After the orchestra's second appearance in the town, the leader presented a substantial check to the Rotary club in appreciation of its action. The money was used by the club for its work with disabled war veterans.

On the other hand, one small act of deceit can strain or rupture the fabric. Even a deceiver can have his confidence shaken. How this can happen is illustrated in this good story told by a Rotarian.

"Let's have breakfast together" had been his response when asked if he could "spare a dime." But when it came time to pay the bill, he discovered to his embarrassment that he had no money with him. "Never mind," said the beggar, "I'll pay for the meal;" and he thereupon produced a crisp five dollar bill. The Rotarian asked him to come home, so that he could be repaid. "No, sir!" cried the beggar. "You fooled me about the breakfast and I'm not going to pay for the taxi."

Two trivial incidents, to be sure, but such as to restore or weaken the invisible sinews of good faith. Small acts do not exist alone and apart. They confirm a habit and furnish an example to discourage or inspire other people.

Vocational service consists not so much in grandiose decisions as in the accumulation of small acts and the slow creation of habits. The little things count.

*In what ways can you
encourage good faith
among your business
or professional associates?*

6

Is Honesty Declining?

THE example of little things is infectious. Often they set in motion curious reactions. One such instance is the story of an American maker of locomotives. He was about to close a large contract with a foreign government. He had stopped over in London before proceeding on to his destination. He was not too happy about the negotiations since it had been decided, at the insistence of the customer, to substitute an inferior grade of steel in order to keep the cost down to a minimum. It seemed the only way in which his firm could secure the contract.

Leaving his London hotel one morning, he noticed in a shop window some material that he thought would make an attractive sports suit. After he had purchased the goods, a London friend gave him the name of a tailor. The American was impressed by the establishment. He was even more impressed when he met the proprietor.

But when the tailor had taken one look at the cloth, to the amazement of the American, he refused to make the suit. He would not put his label on a suit of clothes made of shoddy material. Neither did he respond to the suggestion that since the cloth had already been purchased, the label could be left off in this instance. A tailor could not continue to retain the respect of his employees if he expended their honest labor on dishonest material.

With the bolt of cloth under his arm, the maker of locomotives left the tailor's shop, not angry, but thoughtful. The nameplate on a locomotive, or the label on a suit of clothes, earned respect by the quality of honest labor and honest materials. Unwittingly, the tailor had set him on the right course, as certainly as if he had picked him up physically from one path and set him down upon another.

The first chapter in the "Book of Wisdom," Thomas Jefferson declared, is honesty; and more recently, a well-known editor urged the need for re-establishing the teaching of common honesty in the schools. On the other hand, a school superintendent supporting the affirmative in a debate on the question, "Is Honesty Declining?" placed the responsibility squarely on the shoulders of business. Boys and girls leaving school, he contended, took with them definite standards of honesty and fair play only to be disillusioned by the practices prevailing in places where they worked. "One girl went to work for a dress shop—an exclusive one. As a part of her indoctrination, she was taught three prices for every garment: a top price to be asked first, a middle price, and finally, a minimum. Another lad, when briefed for his part-time work in a grocery store, was told: "Don't be too particular about weights—that is, don't give anything away."

If honesty is not to decline, then home, school, church, trade association, and Rotary club must be alert constantly to combat new tendencies—or fresh manifestations of old tendencies—to chisel and to defraud.

Years ago, Rotary was very active world-wide in the effort to check bribery and secret commissions. A past president of Rotary International represented this interest at an international economic conference of the League of Nations. Many countries enacted legislation to check these evils. "Bribery and secret commissions" —the very words have a musty and antique flavor.

Yet in spite of all these efforts, who can say that bribery and secret commissions are a thing of the past? During and since the war, black markets grew and flourished all over the world. The same gangster elements that furnished the bootleggers during the prohibition era in the United States now appeared as blackmarketeers; the same people who patronized them once, were customers again; and the *same* principle of clandestine corruption was again manifest.

More recently a similar situation was denounced at a district conference of Rotary:

> "We should ask ourselves: 'During recent years when members of all professions were exposed to considerable temptations, have Rotarians succumbed less to these temptations than non-Rotarians?' In all the professions, right from the jeweller to the apple grower, you find, wherever a temptation offered itself, a high price on the back market or an opportunity to pass off inferior quality for superior or the like, the temptation was always succumbed to.
>
> It is a question of character. The trouble is that we look outward and not inwards when it comes to charges of immorality. There are lots of people who, not out of personal greed, but just on account of the fear of being pointed out as simpletons, follow the general line. And to all such people who think that one honest trader, one lawyer who refuses to take dishonest briefs is not going to improve matters, the ancient wisdom of China gives the answer. There is a Chinese proverb which says: 'It is better to light a small candle than to sit cursing the darkness.' "

The same question might be asked with different reference in all the countries which suffered from rising prices and shortages artificially induced.

Could this widespread practice have been checked by vigorous action on the part of trade associations? Or could a strong protest rising from every Rotary club in the world, backed by the example of every Rotarian and his family, have influenced the purchasers and dealers alike to choose the path of strict honesty? Here was an opportunity for vocational service to show its metal and prove its sincerity lest it be classed with those who, in the words of Butler's *Hudibras*—

> Compound for sins they are inclined to,
> By damning those they have no mind to.

The opportunity is still open. The path is plainly marked.

IS HONESTY DECLINING?

Bribery and secret commissions? There is nothing old-fashioned about them at all. They have simply donned modern clothes.

A whiskey salesman sat at a table and ordered a drink. The proprietor followed the waiter and whispered to him: "What did that whiskey salesman order?"

"He ordered one Scotch," said the waiter.

The proprietor then placed three jiggers of rum on the waiter's tray alongside the Scotch, and said: "Tell him that's exactly the way *I* had to buy it!"

What happens one day in a seller's market may recur in reverse order another day when goods become abundant and tie-in sales are replaced by secret rebates, discounts, and presents to buyers.

Laws against bribery and secret commissions are not enough, though they may help to arouse the public conscience. Only the clear, outspoken, and continuous influence of business leaders can be effective, and then only if the leaders have a vital awareness of just what constitutes bribery.

Too often perception is dimmed by reverence for what is done. A court-martial was held in the North African desert to determine the guilt of an Air Force officer charged with accepting bribes from a contractor who had purchased the waste products from the camp.

The most important evidence for the prosecution came from the contractor himself, who admitted without embarrassment that he had paid certain additional sums to secure the right quantity and quality of "swill," but he repudiated indignantly the suggestion that he had received something quite different from swill—a

51

few tins of bully beef, perhaps, cigarettes, or, most important of all tea, coffee, or sugar.

He was a man of character, and he was genuinely shocked at the idea that he would have paid a bribe for something he was not entitled to, though in the ordinary course of business, one paid reasonable bribes to see that business was done properly.

At least such a point of view has the merit of being clear and definite even though it might seem reprehensible in other parts of the world. But frequently polite terms, "customs of the trade" or "pressures from business associates" confuse a man, so that he does not know bribery when he sees it.

Two tests are available, both common-sense, both synonymous with that "sense of community" which spells Rotary. The first is *publicity*. If there is any doubt, for instance, whether a personal gift or a rebate or a price-cut is strictly fair to all concerned, let all concerned know that it is being made. An employer, or a competitor, will be grateful for the information, and the recipient should be flattered to have it known that he is getting this recognition. If the test of publicity arouses embarrassment, then the second and determining test can be applied; that is, whether the gift or other favor tends to raise or lower the level of *service* by this business or profession.

The Rotarian who applies these tests and still finds himself in a gray zone as to what is really the honest course, can seek the council of the vocational service committee of his club or raise the question in his trade association. From the exploration of such gray zones, real progress in raising standards of practice can often result.

IS HONESTY DECLINING?

"Honesty Is the Best Policy" is an opinion that is credited to various writers. Emerson went even further. "Men suffer all their lives from the foolish supposition that they can be cheated. The thief steals from himself. The swindler swindles himself." Honesty is efficient. Dishonesty is laborious, hesitant, and wasteful. This view is emphasized by a curious coincidence in the dictionary definition of *chiseler:* "(1) one who chisels, (2) a child—Ireland." The coincidence of the Irish meaning points to the essential naïvete in all chiseling. Mature people just do not do it.

Surely there is no necessary conflict between idealism and good business. As expanding production fills the gap of previous shortages, many Rotarians may find themselves in the happy position of being able to choose between the alternatives suggested in the following instances:

> A manufacturer put on a special sales drive, and his dealers stocked up. Then without warning, the advertised price on the article was reduced ten per cent. One large dealer reported that he was not even notified. The stores had to wriggle out of the difficulty as best they could. They had bought something at a high price on which they were forced to absorb a ten per cent loss even before they attempted to sell it. Perhaps the manufacturer did not have the price-cut in mind when he caused the stores to increase their inventories. But the dealers said he did.

This incident wrecked more goodwill than heavy expense in advertising could restore in many a month. Contrast with it the policy of another manufacturer in the same field:

> He had moved up production to a point where he was able to cut $20 from the selling-price of a certain model.

Dealers were requested to report the number of machines they had on hand, and checks were sent to them covering the amount of possible loss owing to the price-cut—actual money, not credit on more merchandise.

Is it any wonder that this manufacturer has a loyal and enthusiastic dealer organization?

Is the customer always right? Most men in business have occasion to ponder this slogan at one time or another. A famous department store made a survey which disclosed that there were 75 complaints in every 10, 000 transactions. Consideration was also given to the possibility that many customers did not complain but went elsewhere in future giving the store a bad name among their friends. When salespeople in the store were asked: "Do you believe that it is your job to protect the customer against the store, or the store against the customer?" 99 per cent of them gave the wrong answer.

When it comes to complaints, however, a suspicion sometimes arises whether this slogan is actually true as well as profitable policy. Who is to say whether the customer is really justified in any particular complaint? One Rotarian found an answer that worked satisfactorily. Here it is, in his own words:

"About ten years ago we conceived the idea of allowing our customers to adjust their own complaints. Previous to that time, it had been a poker game. When a customer had a complaint, he would often ask for about twice as much as he expected to get. We would either try to get out of the matter entirely or offer him a quarter of what he asked, and after much wrangling, we would finally agree on some figure.

"By our new methods of making adjustments, the poker playing is eliminated. It is up to the customer to be honest, as we stipulate in making the adjustment that he treat us as he would like to be treated if he were in our place.

"Previous to adopting this policy our adjustments from all causes had run as high as one-and-a-half-per-cent of our sales. The first year after our new policy went into effect, adjustments dropped to three-quarters of one per cent and have been as low as one-twentieth of one per cent."

Is honesty declining? Or, has the business man of today succeeded in removing some of the stigma which once attached to his calling? Was a past president of Rotary International in Great Britain and Ireland correct when he said:

"Until comparatively recent years, the man of business was despised. The only reason was the thought, right or wrong, that meanness, dishonesty, roguery, and often trickery, entered into business transactions. This has only been changed since business men have attempted to put into practice the Golden Rule."

In the growth of confidence, frankness, and consideration between customers, suppliers, and competitors that has replaced the spirit of *"dog-eat-dog"* and *"caveat emptor,"* the Rotarian can gain much encouragement for his efforts to promote honest practices in business or profession. Dishonesty is naïve and ignorant. It can be exposed as such by the success of persistent and resolute example. Perhaps the experience of the salesman who refused to allow an unearned discount is typical. He was invited to pick up the long-distance phone and check with his home office because a very large contract was at stake. But he steadfastly refused. Nothing could persuade him to even question the established policy of his firm.

Suddenly the buyer changed his mind and signed the contract, saying: "A concern that can afford to be so stiff-necked about its own way of doing business, must have a product that can stand on its own merits."

What attitude should be taken towards tipping and seasonal gifts to buyers when they are customary?

7

Is It The Truth?

CONFIDENCE in business is founded on fact and exact statement. Millions upon millions of statements are made every day in all sorts of business situations and by every possible medium of communication. Each occasion is a test of the good faith that relates the individual's integrity to the general prosperity. Of all such occasions, advertising is responsible for the greatest number of statements with the most continuous impact on public confidence. The vast sums spent for advertising—nearly a billion dollars a year in the United States alone—are easily justified by increased volume of sales and consequent employment. More important than costs, however, is the challenge contained in the question that should be applied rigorously by every advertiser to his "copy": *Is it the truth?*

From time to time, a voice is heard crying in the wilderness that there is still adequate selling-power in honest, straightforward advertising. The average man has more common-sense and better taste than the advertiser often credits him with having. People may succumb to the oft-repeated lie as Hitler's *Mein Kampf* so cynically suggested, but slanted statements eventually produce in them apathy and disillusionment. There is a resentful feeling that they are being pushed around. They want desperately to know "what is going on." They are hungry for the truth.

How such feelings may affect the response to advertising was dramatically illustrated in a story told originally in a trade publication and well-known to advertising men. The advertising manager of a department store in Iowa was ill, and his new assistant was doing his best to keep things going. The proprietor, noted for his bluntness of speech, walked into the office.

"Young man," he said, "I want you to stir up some interest in the water-proof garment department. The fact is, we have a lot of raincoats that we've got to get rid of. They are shopworn and some of them are cracked, and we're offering them for little or nothing. Now we've got to get the people to buy them. There are some good ones in the lot, but if we can't sell them, we might as well dump them in the river."

The young man assured the "boss" that he knew exactly how to do it. The next morning the storm broke when the merchant opened his paper to read the store's advertisement for the day. There they were —his own words in bold-face type across the page.

"To tell the truth we have a lot of raincoats we've got to get rid of. They are shopworn and some of them are cracked. We are offering them for little or nothing."

Down went his fist on the table, rattling the dishes, and spilling the coffee.

He read on: "There are some good ones in the lot, but if we can't sell them, we might as well dump them in the river."

Arriving at the store, still fuming, the merchant headed for the advertising office. His partner met him on the way and asked, "Have you heard about the raincoats?"

"Have I? I'm on my way to kick that fool out!"

"Then you haven't heard," remarked his partner. "We couldn't handle the crowd. Every raincoat we advertised was sold thirty minutes after we opened. That advertisement was a wonder. Seemed to please people by its absolute frankness."

The chance remark of an attorney in an American courtroom had wide repercussions. It ignited the spark of a great movement. Brushing off a charge of inaccuracy, he was heard to say: "Why of course all advertising is exaggerated. Nobody really believes it."

The utter absurdity of this statement impressed a listener in the courtroom. If nobody really believes it, what's the use of advertising? Yet, every exaggeration or distortion of fact does indeed tend to destroy confidence, not only in the advertisement but in all advertising and all business. The millions of dollars spent in advertising are wasted if nobody believes it. So began a long and successful campaign for truth in advertising that led eventually to the Better Business Bureau with its organized effort to unmask fraud and deception.

Truth is the primary purpose of the Better Business Bureau. Truth is its weapon. The local branches of the bureau do not prosecute the swindler or the deceptive advertiser. They merely expose him. Investigation—analysis—publicity—is the sequence which brings truth to light, and forces him to desist or retract publicly. Extensive records are kept by the bureaus for the protection of investors, customers, and newspapers who might be involved. Through these powerful means, Better Business Bureaus in nearly a hundred cities of the United States are protecting the reputation of legitimate business and helping to sustain the credibility of all advertising. Many Rotary clubs have helped to bring them into existence. Many Rotarians are active as managers or as members of their local boards.

Volumes would be required to catalogue the tricks —some crude, some subtle—through which advertising deviates from the truth. One common kind of deception was illustrated in the radio program of the American comedians, Amos and Andy. Exultantly, Andy brought home a fraudulent insurance policy, impressive with its gold seal and blue ribbon. It promised a thousand dollars to his heirs. Amos examined the policy carefully, and then remarked sadly: "It's no good,

IS IT THE TRUTH?

Andy. The big type gives it to you; and the little type takes it away."

Business men whose behavior in their personal transactions is above suspicion succumb sometimes to a sort of poetic or artistic license when it comes to approving advertisements. Only a constant zeal for truth can make them alert to discern possible deviations. The following questions may help Rotarians to detect some of the misleading devices that creep into advertisements:

Is the format of the advertisement used to underplay important, but less attractive aspects, of the business offer?

Do pictures or descriptive phrases used, give an objective description of the article?

Are terms like "scientific proof," "cold facts," "inside figures" used to bolster loose statements?

Are testimonials by celebrities in other fields honest evidence of technical superiority?

Should paid testimonials be used?

Do comparative statements such as "formerly $10" or "up to $100 values" describe exactly the reduction in prices of individual articles that has occurred?

Is every person concerned with issuing the advertisement thoroughly aware of his responsibility to the whole public?

The responsibility of advertising is to inform the customer so that he may purchase more intelligently. This purpose is not accomplished by claims or implications that the advertiser is underselling his competitors. Such aspersions are as unfair in respect of competitor relations as they are generally inaccurate and misleading. They cannot always be exposed, however, as readily as was the salesman who boasted that "our paint is used on eighty per cent of the cars in America."

Impatiently the buyer interrupted him: "Your rival says in his catalogue that his paint is used on seventy per cent."

"What did I tell you?" retorted the salesman. "We've got him beat by ten per cent."

Comparisons are stupid as well as odious if they distract attention from the merits of the product advertised. Yet, how often this happens. Two well-known department stores condescended to berate each other recently over the merits of a new style of fountain pen. One store advertised that it had been the "first in the world" with the great invention. The other swung back: "Do you own a horse and buggy model?" Next week, the reply came: "When Johnny-come-lately tries to put Johnny-on-the-spot on the spot, what happens?" All very clever and amusing, but hardly encouraging to the customer, whose confidence in the product ebbed with the rising tide of competing recriminations.

Of course, there is no way of drawing up a balance-sheet to show the losses to advertisers as a whole that result from misleading advertisements. The incident of the shopworn raincoats was a parable—even though it actually occurred. The misleading advertiser may trade for a while on the confidence created by others, but his reputation is likely to suffer more than theirs, so that in the end it will not pay him to advertise at all. Indeed, there is evidence that in actual practice crooked business shuns publicity of any kind.

But advertising after all is only one phase of business —an echo which translates into public expression the pitch of integrity attained in plant and office and other departments. The echo rebounds from one department to another. A concern which tries to fool others is likely to end by fooling itself. If the advertisement is untrustworthy, what can be expected of the salesman's expense account or the stockroom inventory? If the pitch is false throughout, it can mean ruin.

Many business men have realized the critical importance of integrity throughout their organizations by making this question, "Is it the truth?"—a test for every decision and transaction in their business. They have instructed every employee to use it habitually. They have not allowed the shifting sands of fashion nor the clamor of competition to divert them from the need for plain facts and exact statements in every business relationship. They know that it pays to be truthful. Nor are they disturbed in this conviction by the play of subtle minds. "What is truth?" said jesting Pilate, and would not stay for an answer. The answer is clear enough, for it is not honest error, but deliberate misstatement and misrepresentation, that destroy confidence.

It is told of Socrates that one day when he was bathing, a young man came to him and said, "Master, I have traveled a long distance to see you. Will you teach me what is Truth?"

Socrates invited him into the water; then put his head under and held it there until the young man struggled and gasped for breath. When he indignantly demanded to know the reason for such treatment, Socrates replied: "When you want Truth as much as you wanted air just now, you will find it."

A passion for truth in every detail and every aspect of the daily round in business or profession can only be cultivated slowly and methodically. Yet how much the business or profession will benefit from it! Once the subterfuges and misrepresentations are swept ruthlessly away, good faith and confidence will lay open the path to greater service.

How could your club help
to improve the standards
of advertising in its
trading area?

8

Pioneers in Human Relations

Anyone interested in improving his human relations has much to learn from the art of salesmanship as it has developed through the years. To begin with, the operation of selling is almost universal. The human relations of professional men, for instance, are largely with patients or clients—customers, if you please of their services. Every producer must seek a market, even if it be through an employment office or an advertising column or a business letter. To the schoolteacher, the pupil or the parent may well be represented as a purchasing agent. Even the clergyman has a selling job to do. Selling is a two-way process: a buyer is also involved, and all people are buyers. The mistakes, the temptations, and the insights of salesmen are present to some extent in all these occupations.

Salesmen, furthermore, have had the courage to recognize their mistakes. More intensive study has been made of the problems in selling than in any other field of human relations. Much can be learned from these pioneers.

Why do people buy? *What* do customers want, actually? *How* is the salesman equipped to satisfy these wants? Even those whose occupation is far removed from selling can apply these questions to their relations with business or professional associates.

Why do people buy? There is no denying that price is a great consideration. A recent survey in the United States showed the importance of impulse buying, the kind of buying people do when they happen to see something that appeals to them and decide to buy it on the spot. Fifty-three per cent of all purchases in chain stores is impulse buying. Forty-two per cent of department-store business, and even twenty-four per cent of grocery purchases come from buying on the impulse. Nothing freezes an impulse so much as high prices.

Prices, however, are by no means the whole story. People desire quality, too. Often they are apt to think that quality makes an article economical at a higher price. A salesman who was encountering among his prospects a good deal of price resistance found that a frank admission was his best approach.

"Our service is not intended for any but the better rugs," was his initial statement. "I have called on you because I understand that you are the owner of very good rugs . . ." If the lady of the house did not agree that her rugs were better than most people's, the salesman gracefully withdrew, because he could spend his time to better advantage talking to other prospects who *were* interested in quality.

But more important even than price or quality is imagination—imagination of the circumstances, the needs, the motivations of the buyer. *"Were You Mistaken?"* was the arresting caption of an advertisement in a Rotary club publication, which read: "So you thought we were jewelers! Well, well, does it not beat all how these ideas seem to get around. Just because our vaults are bulging wide with diamonds and precious stones, with quaint and beautiful pieces of gold and silver and platinum (and because we have mentioned it from time to time) you naturally jumped to the conclusion that our only business was selling jewels. And now we have to tell you that you were perhaps mistaken. What we really sell is something quite different than you think. We sell the most precious, the most fragile, the most beautiful things in all this world. We sell Love. We sell Romance. We sell Adventure. We sell Loyalty that lasts through the years undisturbed by time and tide . . . We traffic in old-fashioned gardens with great hedges of lilacs. We are guardians of your Memories, the makers of the only dreams that last." And so on to the genial conclusion: "Everything else in time grows old but love and truth, and jewels."

Who would dispute the insight of this advertisement into the real desires of the prospective customers?

l'earls of greatest price are those personal associations which they wish to commemorate.

A salesman who has the imagination to project himself into the mind of another person to discover his real needs performs a high function, for often the other person is not quite aware of them himself. The salesman is able to crystallize vague desires perhaps, or he actually creates a value not intrinsic in his product, but none the less real since it was born of the salesman's sincere interest and perception.

How much better for the salesman to study the actual needs of his customers than to try to get business by mere assertion of his own will and desire for an order. Baked beans were a drug on the market in one city where the housewives had the habit of baking their own. All the rival manufacturers had done was to clamor: "Buy my brand!"

Then one of them had the imagination to present the housewife's side of the picture. His advertisements told of the sixteen hours required to bake beans at home and why home-baking could never make the beans digestible. He pictured home-baked beans with the crisp beans on top, the mushy ones below. Then he showed how the factory selected their beans, used soft water, and steam ovens. A free sample was offered for comparison. The customer was even invited to "Try Our Rivals', Too!"

Success attended this selling campaign because the salesman did not argue anything for his own advantage, but unselfishly considered the needs of his prospective customers. People respond to the unselfish, imaginative approach—by purchasing.

What do customers want, actually? First and foremost, they want to make up their own minds. They do not want to be browbeaten or tricked or persuaded. They want information that enables them to decide for themselves. The salesman has to let them buy. They cannot be sold.

The salesman who sets out to provide the needed information as lucidly, conveniently, and completely as he can, is the successful salesman. A store that gives the impression of placing all its cards on the table, face up, receives the gratitude of the customers and their respect. They feel that no available information is being concealed when every article has the price plainly marked, and when they are able to wander about making up their own minds without the hot breath of the salesman forever hounding them for a decision. Oh yes, they want him within reach ready to answer their questions, to share his experience, and to help them make comparisons. But he is wanted as a friend, not as an antagonist, as someone they can trust to furnish an authentic background for their purchases.

At a time when technology is mutiplying the supply of goods available, the estimate that 70 per cent of sales lost result from indifference on the part of salespeople assumes an importance vital to the whole economy. When questioned about their product or service, they are prone to shrug their shoulders as if to say: "Don't ask me. I just work here." Or they are like the salesman who offered a fine pair of shoes priced accordingly. To try him out, the customer exclaimed: "That's highway robbery!" Did the salesman tell him that he had other good shoes for less, but this was the finest produced? Did he point to the additional costs in manufacturing quality shoes? Not at all. He blamed the manufacturer for "holding us up" in a tone which implied: "That's your problem. I couldn't care less." Such indifference is a sure way to irritate a potential purchaser and to frustrate all the ingenuity and passion for perfection that has gone into the production of the goods. Only a genuine interest in the products and a genuine desire to help the customer equip salespeople to play their vital part in an expanding economy.

Salesmen who go out of their way to teach customers how to make better use of products or get longer wear from them may lose immediate sales, but they are watering the delicate flower of confidence which blossoms in repeat orders—the most profitable kind of business. A wire-brush manufacturer found a way to double the service of a brush used extensively on a certain kind of polishing-machine. So he made a point of visiting every purchaser of this brush to show him personally how the saving could be accomplished. It looked like plain suicide for the manufacturer, but these visits enabled him to demonstrate also other uses for his brushes. He clinched many profitable accounts and profitable repeat business followed. This was not plain suicide, but the salvaging of a threatened relationship, for, sooner or later, someone else would have discovered the saving and confidence in the manufacturer might have been shaken.

Like the fabulous Janus of Roman mythology, the salesman is always looking in two directions to improve his knowledge of what people want. He is the channel of information that conveys the needs and desires of the consumer to the producer, as well as a source of expert knowledge to the buyer.

Such, ideally, is the vocation of the salesman when he is convinced that service is his business. But actually . . . ? *How* does the salesman become equipped to satisfy the needs of customers?

Training—specialized training—is the answer. The employer of the salesman should be his teacher. To be a teacher, the employer should be utterly genuine. If he is thinking of profit rather than service—if he is putting pressure on his salesmen to "produce"—then his attitude will be reflected in the salesman, whatever the teaching.

The employer who is genuinely interested in improved service can inspire his salesman with that sincere interest in people and their needs which spells successful selling. The salesman will be trained, not to win arguments, but to ask questions—to make the other person feel that *he* is the important factor in the transaction.

The salesman will be trained as an expert in his line, as a mine of technical information about the background of his products—not for arrogant display, but as necessary equipment for feeling his way toward the actual needs and interests of the customer. An old lady listened patiently to the long sales talk that a clerk had memorized. Overwhelmingly, he set forth all the fine points of a stove, its many "gadgets," its chromium plating, and the like.

At last, timidly, as he paused for breath, she ventured a question: "Will it keep an old lady warm?"

No small part of the salesman's training comes from

his experience with customers. Arrogance, insincerity, and downright deceitfulness may and often do merely reflect the kind of reception accorded the salesman by those whom he aspires to serve. It is uphill work for

---

Welcome!

MR. SALESMAN

YOU will receive courteous attention here, for we are mindful that our own salesmen are making their calls every day, seeking interviews and business just as you are.

WE are glad to have you call, because it is an important part of our business to keep in touch with new developments and changes in products and services. Can you tell us something new . . . something we should know . . . or show us how your goods or services can help us do a better job?

WE know how much our salesmen appreciate a cordial welcome from their customers and prospects. And because we believe that the practice of the Golden Rule should begin at home, we shall keep you waiting no longer than is absolutely necessary.

Thank you for coming to see us!

---

him to develop a wholehearted devotion to the interests of his customers if they snub him, keep him waiting fruitlessly, and behave generally as if he were an enemy and a bore to boot. Like begets like. The customer who shuts himself off from these sources of information is not serving his own interests. He is needlessly increasing the cost of serving him. He is failing to realize that buying and selling are operations, not opposite in character but essentially alike, *combined* operations to achieve more efficient distribution.

Reproduced here is a card which is prominently displayed at the receptionist's desk of a company that interviews many salesmen. How encouraging to the salesman a visit to this organization must be. So much depends on atmosphere in a business or in a town. Every gesture of courtesy lights a torch that is passed from hand to hand, lighting for each one, new vistas of opportunity for better human relations and greater service.

What has been said about the salesman's problems and purposes applies to the buyer in equal measure. He, too, is vitally concerned to secure a source of supply on which he can depend. His main function is also the provision of accurate information to his source about his plans and problems, so that together they can work out solutions beneficial to all concerned. If all the facts cannot be disclosed by the buyer, at least he will be frank in admitting it. He will never attempt to mislead the salesman by exaggerations, hedging or half-truths, for such insincerity is fatal to the atmosphere of cordial co-operation which is his chief aim.

In the creation of this atmosphere, Rotarians can play a great part, not only by their personal conduct and influence, but through club activities. An interesting attempt to get Rotarians to look into the mirror —as employers, as salesmen, and as buyers—was made in a Rotary program where a salesman and a purchasing agent tore the problem of their mutual relations apart in terms of "My Pet Peeves" and "The Kind I Like." As members of the club joined the discussion, a richer understanding of the common task of these two vocations emerged.

The same idea is stimulated by another Rotary club which sponsors a so-called "peddlers' picnic" to which each member invites a salesman for a day of better acquaintance and jollity at the country club. Or there is the project of a "courtesy contest" undertaken in many towns by Rotary clubs which offer prizes for letters describing special acts of service by salespeople. Any Rotarian can make it his business to suggest projects of this kind to his club, and any club that undertakes them can be sure that the effects will be far-reaching.

An unexpected result of a courtesy contest, for instance, was that several local firms and a hospital started courtesy contests of their own for their employees. The town as a whole became conscious of the possibilities for improvement in human relations, and the results quickly became apparent to visitors from other towns.

What steps are you taking to improve your buying and selling relationships?

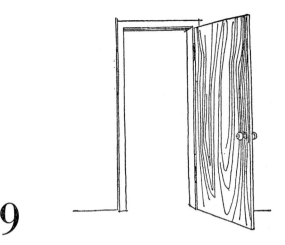

9

Channels of Communication

COMMUNICATION is the magic mockery that science makes of distance. Swift flight has brought any spot of the globe within sixty hours' travel from "our town." The minds of men are being linked across the planet by telephone, radio, and television while a closely co-ordinated system of transport brings the loneliest farm within the reach of civilization.

Through highly sensitive devices, marvels of ingenuity and discipline, this conquest of distance is achieved. Yet the conqueror himself, too often remains isolated in spirit, aloof from his fellow-men, incapable of the most rudimentary gesture or contact.

As we have seen, an essential element in service consists in bridging the gulf created by self-interest. In the case of a competitor, it meant going more than half-way in friendship. Where customers were concerned, real communication was established through the sales-man's interest in their actual needs.

Not so evident, however, is the need for dispelling the distance that authority interposes in relations with employees. Subconsciously a distinction is made be-tween customers who are wooed with every sort of con-sideration—and employees whose time, talents, and energies have been purchased and brought under au-thority. According to the common assumption, it is the employee's role to woo the favor of the man who has hired him.

There is usually a half-truth in most common as-sumptions that need not be denied while the whole truth is being sought. Granting the authority of the employer—even in a period of acute labor shortage—is it not true likewise that employees are just as vital to the success of a business as customers? He profits most . . . whose employees are alert, intelligent, and co-operative. If they are lackadaisical clockwatchers, their employer may be wasting as much as fifty per cent of his annual payroll. If they are discontented and rebel-lious, all the profit from his skillful organization may go with the wind.

Once the employee is hired, moreover, there is a change in the relationship. The employer ceases to be merely the purchaser of a commodity. He becomes in some respects a salesman, with the employee in the position of a customer who has to be "sold" on his job

—instructed and inspired to co-operate with a whole heart. Even though the employee who proves unsatisfactory can be dismissed, his case is not so different from that of a customer whose account is closed for one reason or another.

Much of the experience gained in relations with customers can be applied in obtaining the best efforts from employees. The first step is to overcome the distance imposed by authority. The salesman finds that his primary function is to study the needs of his customers and to place their interest in satisfactory service before his own interest in profit. Customers respond favorably to such treatment, and so do employees.

"They act as though they wanted to give us a break," said the president of a trade-union in tribute to a company with which he had been having difficult negotiations. "We don't always win, but no matter how big or how small the matter may be, they always listen. You can't help liking guys who listen."

The lack of easy channels of communication is often an initial cause of many destructive labor disputes that spread impoverishment far and wide. Inability to listen is no less fatal in many small businesses where silent frustration may be even more destructive of efficiency than open revolt. Rotary in action would provide an open door to the boss's office, a standing invitation to employees to come in and air their difficulties. The president of a Rotary club in California suggests the following points to remember "when an employee is dissatisfied and comes to you for an interview":

Listen, don't talk. Many things will work themselves

out when the employee is allowed to "get it off his chest."

Don't argue.

Don't lecture. The employee feels cut off. Lecturing blocks communication.

Pay attention to what he wants to say and help him to express himself clearly.

Don't express moral attitudes.

Don't let your emotions creep in.

Test your understanding and at the same time stimulate further expression by summarizing from time to time the employee's views.

The employer's effort in all such interviews should be to help the employee talk out his problem; to secure an understanding of the difficulty; and to assist in finding a solution.

The precious time given to such interviews will not be wasted if they result in a new awareness and increased energy on the part of the employee. Without pretending to be psychiatrists, employers need not ignore the fact that personality problems often affect the efficiency of the worker. These may spring from tangible worries ranging from sickness in the home to unpleasant relations with a fellow-employee. Or, it may be some deep-seated personal difficulty.

A doctor who has had much experience with the impact of personality in factory work has classified these maladjustments as arising from a number of causes: excessive preoccupation with self, aggressive responses to things or persons in the environment, aggressions turned inward (often resulting in deliber-

78

ate accidents, drunkenness, or self-induced failure) passively dependent traits, and compensation for insecurity or inadequacy.

The employer who thinks he detects any of these maladjustments in his employees may not be able to provide a complete solution. Knowledge of their existence, however, may suggest changes in the kind of work the employee is doing or perhaps association with different people.

Praise and blame are two channels of communication open directly to the employer because of his authority. Used positively, constructively, in relation to performance of the job rather than to personality— both can bring about a better relationship with employees. Blame, however impersonal, may be depressing unless the recipient is very sure of his ability to overcome the defect. Many employers accordingly prefer "a criticism sandwich"—two slices of praise for things the employee is actually accomplishing with one slice of blame in between where correction is desired or needed. In keeping blame impersonal, complete privacy is almost essential, for spectators direct the employee's attention toward himself and create a feeling of self-pity.

An employer, moreover, who takes upon his own shoulders a generous share of the blame for failures that have occurred not only avoids humiliating the worker, but also discourages any tendency to "pass the buck," a habit as infectious as it is harmful to the general morale of the business.

Is there any substantial reason for the fear sometimes expressed that such human consideration for the feelings of employees detracts from the authority and dignity of the boss? Surely not. There is no question here of "coddling" employees any more than might exist in a similar concern for the feelings and complaints of customers. The same Golden Rule impels you to treat employees as you would like to be treated if you yourself were working at the bench or behind the counter.

Each complaint provides an opportunity for achieving basic improvements in the relationship. Rules that are infringed may need to be explained or it may develop that they are not really necessary. Employers are discovering constantly that the abolition of needless restrictions is very helpful to employee morale, and that self-discipline or group discipline by fellow-workers is just as effective. A plant that dispensed with time-clocks and permitted the employees to smoke, lunch, or rest when they chose, was rewarded by increased output. Abuse of these privileges by individual workers was roundly rebuked by fellow-workers. An "honor-system" shifted the burden of unpleasant supervision to the employees themselves.

Another valuable channel of communication is the encouragement of new ideas and suggestions. A labor leader gave trenchant utterance to the need for opening this channel. "There never was a factory yet that came within hailing distance of its fullest possible production," he told his union members. "And it never will without *you* and *you* and *you*. You can see things that management can't see. You can see the little wastes that add up to the one great terrible waste. Management can't stop them. You can."

CHANNELS OF COMMUNICATION

An employee should know the details of his job better than anyone else. Certainly, he has a particular point of view and a special interest in it. Ideas often occur to him that would escape anyone not so closely identified with the work at hand. If he knows that his suggestions are welcomed, carefully studied, and fairly rewarded—or, at the least, recognized—he is likely to take a more intelligent attitude toward his work.

A railroad has popularized the slogan, "There is no ceiling on new ideas." In its advertising it boasts of the thousands of dollars it has paid for valuable employee suggestions. No matter if three-fourths of the ideas prove impractical—provided their authors are told why—those that are adopted more than compensate for the trouble of installing a suggestion system. The value of the by-products in general keenness and sense of participation is inestimable. No concern is so small that it cannot benefit from a system that employees know is fair and efficient.

A broadening of this channel of communication has been introduced by a Rotarian in what he calls "multiple management." In his business, a revolving committee of employees considers suggestions for improved efficiency with the single stipulation that they must approve ideas unanimously before endorsing them. Very few of the proposals endorsed by these committees have failed to receive prompt and profitable application. In addition, there has been instilled throughout the concern a spirit that could not be purchased at any price. As one employee put it, "I feel like I'm in business for myself with someone else's money."

One leading British company has a meeting every three or four weeks with a group of employees whose names literally come out of the hat and represent all departments. No minutes are taken and the directors present give a guarantee that no employee will be penalized in any way for anything he may say. Only one question is asked by management: "What's wrong with us, and how do you think we can improve our management of the company?"

The results are reported to be immensely worth while, and the directors have gained a valuable personal contact with large numbers of their workpeople by this means. Great interest has been created in the progress and management of the concern, and during the operation of the plan over a number of years there have been no strikes.

Employees too often assume that management knows little or nothing of their problems. However, a recent study of the largest businesses in America showed that the starting wages of the 143 men who are now top executives averaged $13.40 a week. Like the vast majority of employers, these men started very near the bottom. Yet to how many employees, is management away off somewhere in an ivory tower?

Similarly, the wildest opinions often exist about the extent of profit that is being taken from industry. One poll of workers registered the belief that the owners took seventy-five per cent of the gross receipts. Railroad employees guessed on the average that stockholders of their road received a twenty-seven per cent return on their investment, whereas the actual dividends amounted to just three per cent. Another poll of workers revealed that less than a quarter of those polled had received any substantial information about the plans and prospects, problems or profits of the concerns which employed them.

Does not this failure to communicate, rather than any ambition on the part of employees to usurp the functions of management, explain much current discontent and unrest?

Many alternative channels exist for dispelling this kind of ignorance. Some firms enclose in their pay envelopes simple and graphic statements of their financial situation. Others make such statements a part of the general information in house organs which are distributed to employees and their families. Smaller concerns may best convey this information through meetings of employers with employees.

The object of such meetings should be to reduce the distance imposed by authority; to impart the fervor that may be lost in transmission through subordinates; and to face frankly the problems and misunderstandings that disturb employees. The Rotarian who is able to do this with simplicity and without, as one executive put it, "making noises like a corporation," has not wasted his Rotary training.

In many parts of the world, these meetings are organized permanently as a "works council" in which representatives of the employees are invited to discuss the problems and the progress of the business. British Rotarians claim success in overcoming a suspicion among the workers that the works council is "just another dodge to pull the wool over their eyes." Constant presence of the chief executive of the business at meetings of the works council, alternating chairmanship between employees and management, complete equality for all in candid expressions of opinion are among the remedies for such feelings.

The scope of the idea is indicated by its adaptation to the needs of natives engaged in industry as reported by Rotarians in South Africa:

> The eyes of the world are focused on South Africa and its native policy more now than at any time of its history. We must be progressive in our thoughts on this issue generally although our specific interest is with the native in our own industry.
>
> The procedure for the establishment of a native works council is simple in the extreme. Avoid a constitution and do not bar discussion on any subject. Two or three members of the management should be on the council with any number of Africans. Meet at monthly intervals and never hesitate to call special meetings. Members should hold office for twelve months and should not be elected on a tribal basis.
>
> Employees elect their own members to serve on the works council. Sitting around a table with the chairman of the board of directors, they hammer out all their difficulties, and often make valuable suggestions for the betterment of the firm.
>
> I can honestly say that the effect of these works councils has been most marked, and not in one instance has it failed to prevent employees going out on strike.

To give all employees a clear picture of the council's work, Rotarians recommend publication of the full minutes of its meetings. A booklet issued by one firm under the title of, *What It Has Done,* credited the council with first-rate ideas on production, the reduction of absenteeism, and the creation of a more friendly atmosphere in the plant.

Besides being prolific in valuable suggestions for improved efficiency, works councils often concern themselves with the general welfare and health of employees, savings and benefit funds, improvements in safety, or projects for entertainment and education. Above all, they contribute to a feeling of responsibility and self-respect in every worker by giving him a sense of belonging to the "team."

Meetings with employees also provide the best atmosphere for communicating the ideals of vocational service. This good thing should be shared. If a Rotarian keeps Rotary to himself as a private cult, he is missing much of his opportunity to serve society. The daily incidents of business furnish him with admirable illustrations for arousing in his associates the realization that "they also serve." It will interest them to know why he goes each week to his Rotary meeting, what he gets there, and how it affects them. No better bridge could be constructed for human relations than the explanation by an employer of his own adventure in service. And how thrilling to his employees would be his invitation to comradeship in this adventure.

"They also serve." The eagerness of employees to share, richly and deeply, the aims which Rotary brings to business, has been amply demonstrated. Here, for instance, is the experience of a Rotarian who employs a total of seven persons. One day, he called all seven of them together, told them something of the vocational service program of Rotary and then presented to each

SERVICE IS MY BUSINESS

of them a copy of "Service is My Business" with the suggestion that he would like to have them read the book at their convenience.

Only Sam, an old negro who had worked many years as a general handyman did not get a copy, for he had never learned to read. A copy was presented, however, to Sam's son who worked part-time in the store.

A few days later, the Rotarian heard that Sam had asked his son to read the book aloud to him. Questioned about it, Sam replied: "Yassuh, we not only read it through once, but we has almost finished it twiced."

"Did you, indeed? Well, just what does the book mean to you?"

"Why, suh," replied Sam, "I got this much out of it; it don't make no difference how good those manu-facturers make those drugs we got here in the store or how good they make those oxygen tents, if ol' Sam don't get them delivered to the right place and in time, they aren't goin' to be worth nothin' at all."

*What are you doing to make
your employees aware of
the purposes of Rotary?*

10

A Square Deal for Employees

THE contract, express or implied, which ties a man to his job is one in which good faith must have the deepest significance. From the employer's standpoint, the work done within his business is the commodity he offers to society. Faithful work is essential to the success of the business—faithful employees its greatest asset.

For the employee, this contract concerns the most precious of all commodities—his own life—which he invests in the organization that employs him. His past experience, present status, and future hopes are all packaged in this fateful agreement. If he does not have confidence that he is "getting a square deal" in return for his outlay of energy and skill, he suffers a deep frustration that may be harmful to his efficiency.

The question of a person's worth is not determined, of course, by the whim or benevolence of the employer. A cartoon pictures a bar of iron worth $5.00. The same bar of iron made into horseshoes would be worth $10.50. Made into needles, it has a value of $3,285.00; and if turned into balance-springs for watches, it becomes worth $250,000.00. The value of any material is not determined so much by what is in it as by the *service* it performs.

So it is with people. Their economic value depends on what they produce. This, in turn, depends upon a great many complicated considerations. Only under the most primitive conditions of production and barter might the worker hope to get the full value of his production. In the Middle Ages, the problem was already so complex that theologians argued endlessly over the just wage and the just price. Today, with machine production, fluctuating currencies, and the extreme specialization that separates the producer from the ultimate consumer, the problem of what is a just wage in any particular instance becomes practically insoluble.

The president of a Brazilian Rotary club, in an address on employee relations, expressed part of the dilemma as follows:

> The principle is that it does not appear to be right to fix the same remuneration for good and bad elements alike, and to lose sight of the immediate aim of a salary which should correspond to the work produced. We admit that the minimum wage was a necessity to avoid abuses. But from there onward, the actual system of increasing wages under threats, or under impositions, in-

cluding prosperous concerns with those of smaller resources, comes to be a crying inequality.

The difficulty of actually achieving a square deal
with employees only increases the need for *good faith
in seeking one.* An open and earnest effort to establish
a fair scale of rewards is needed. But, in describing the
efforts of some Rotarians, no claim is made that any
one of them actually achieves a square deal or that a
specific plan could be used in every business. They are
reported, rather, as manifestations of good faith and
sincere intention.

Each business has its own special problems and must
cut its coat according to its cloth.

The modern sciences of aptitude-testing and job-
analysis are useful in finding the relative worth of em·
ployees in the same business. Keeping square pegs out
of round holes, and making sure that each task is
valued correctly in terms of difficulty and experience
does not determine, however, what wages should be
paid. At best, human abilities are conserved with resulting benefit to all concerned.

A Swiss Rotarian was able to develop a simple plan
for determining wages in a plant where there had been
many complaints and jealousies among the workers. A
basic wage was graduated according to the age and domestic responsibilities of the worker. To this was added
a so-called active wage based on the degree of skill or
experience required by the particular job. In addition,
a productive wage was geared to output. Since each
part of the plan was assessed on a common point system, the satisfaction of the workers arose from knowing
exactly what was required to improve their position.

A rather similar point system is used by an American insurance company to decide the readiness of its employees for promotion. The following qualities are taken into consideration: teachability, supervisory responsibility, initiative, public relations, analytical ability, personal friendliness, monetary responsibility, application, volume of work, neatness and accuracy, thoroughness.

Each quality (teachability, for example) is assessed according to the following definitions, and the capacity for advancement emerges from the average score after all the qualities have been assessed.

	SCORE
Needs repeated instruction (unsatisfactory in present position)	1
Requires detailed instruction (decreasing efficiency)	2
Slightly below average (keep in present position)..	3
Average (advance questionable)	4
Slightly above average (advance slowly)	5
Readily grasps new ideas (advance steadily)	6
Outstanding ability (advance rapidly)	7

An obvious weakness of this system is the variability of human capacities and the relative importance of particular qualities to any given job. The chief advantage, however, is in making such assessments known to the employee. In this way he may see where improvement is needed and be convinced of the good faith of his employer and that he is receiving a square deal. Many Rotarians take pride in the fact that their good faith with employees is so evident, and working conditions so satisfactory, that no employee has ever been moved to ask for a raise.

It would be ideal if ambition could be directed always into constructive effort through the assurance that increased productivity would reflect automatically in the pay check. The National Industrial Conference Board (U.S.A.) offered a critical study of "measured day work." A base rate of pay was established after a job had been valued in terms of complexity, skill, mental, and physical demands. This rate was then compared with prevailing rates for similar jobs in the same area. In addition, extra compensation ranging from 15 per cent to 25 per cent of the measured day rate was given for production, quality, versatility, and dependability. One result of this plan has been less spoilage, because the worker knows that each piece of scrap affects his rating. There is also an eagerness to develop short cuts in manufacturing, and closer relations with supervisors.

One disadvantage noted in this plan is that exceptionally fast workers are discouraged by the limited variation between normal and maximum rates. That weakness was overcome by a Rotarian who operates a factory with fifty employees. He made them virtual sub-contractors of the orders which came into the plant. The employer furnished the material and machines, and bore the overhead expense. The worker supplied his labor at a rate considered fair to him, to the company, and to the customer. From the moment this sub-contract was accepted, the worker became his own boss. The faster he worked, the more orders he could handle and the higher his wages would climb.

This scheme was profitable to the company because it permitted exact cost control, and the results in employee satisfaction were amazing. Not only did ambition lead to greatly increased earnings, but there was no need for pushing or for stop-watch holding and little need for inspection because a spoiled unit had to be done over on the employee's own time.

There is ample evidence that thorough development of such plans is beneficial to all concerned. Another company with an incentive-pay plan reported an 80 per cent decrease in man-hours for the same volume of goods, a $5,000 annual wage for laboring men, lower prices to the customer, and dividends on a stable basis from year to year for the stockholders.

Business stability interests not only stockholders but everyone affected by the boom-and-bust cycle that has plagued world economy. Most affected of all is the employee who is laid off during slack times. One man so affected strode into the office of his Rotarian employer.

"You can't do this to me!" he declared bluntly. "You can't turn me out onto the street. You wouldn't do that to a horse. You can't do it to me."

The employer was embarrassed. "Can't you go back to the job you came from?" he asked.

"No, I can't," said the man. "I had just got a little business started when you sent a man to ask me to work for you. I didn't know that you would just keep me a couple of months—just long enough to ruin my business—and then turn me out."

This caused the Rotarian to think hard. His business was of a seasonal nature, and such layoffs were quite common and customary. But were they *fair to all con-*

cerned? By careful planning, he was able to reorganize his operations so that every employee was hired at an annual wage. The key to his plan was flexibility. New employees were assigned to an "extra gang" which fills in wherever there is a rush. Whole departments were organized as extra gangs. In this way, it was possible to keep his labor force busy and earning most of the year.

That this plan, coupled with an incentive system on a departmental basis and profit-sharing, is satisfactory to labor is evidenced by the recent renewal of a union contract which included a guaranteed annual wage for 2,080 hours each year. Actually this type of contract is being sought increasingly by trade-unions, and a U.S.A. government study indicates that introducing these features in most seasonal industries would not increase costs more than six per cent if co-ordinated with existing system of state unemployment compensation. While no panacea for insecurity, this study concluded, the annual wage does make a substantial contribution to the stabilization of purchasing power.

How purchasing power can be "stabilized" was described at a Christmas party in an American pottery plant where the owner, who had been on poor relief 14 years previously, distributed $705,000 to his 827 employees. Each of the 88 men and women who had been with the business ten years or more received a bonus of $3,500. This story-book rise to riches began when the employer with seven other relief clients came to live in an abandoned pottery building. "My road has not been an easy one," remarked the employer to his party guests, "but no man could ask for one more pleasant. Many people would like to be a king, possess great riches, or live a life of ease, but I would not trade your friendship for anything in the world."

This story has a heart-warming sequel. More than a year later, a disastrous fire left half the pottery a charred and twisted ruin. Uninsured, the owner thought that he was ruined, but he had not counted on his friends. While the building still smoldered, hundreds of employees and townsfolk were at work feverishly clearing away the debris. Manufacturers of materials were promising quick delivery. To show that he could count on them, employees put $1,000 into a pot before the fire was out, and subsequently worked at a low hourly rate on the unfamiliar task of rebuilding. Within two months, the plant was restored and equipped for a greater volume of production. Once more the employer had an apt comment: "I've invested in human nature in this community and no man ever received greater profits than its goodwill."

The theme of "you can't take it with you" has often been a dominant note in profit-sharing, but the aim of giving employees a square deal and actually increasing profits through stimulating their keenness, inspires the more carefully thought-out plans. Whether as largess, as a demonstration of good faith, or as plain good business, the tangible participation of employees in the success of capitalist enterprise is receiving widespread attention.

The Eastern Rotary Wheel reports a club meeting in Calcutta, India, where profit-sharing was seen as the cure for labor conflict, particularly in small concerns where there is intimate contact between all sections. Under the New Zealand Company Act (1924 and 1933) a plan for "labor shares" designed by a Rotarian became legal. In this scheme of employee-partnership, control of the business as well as profits is assigned on the basis of personal service. Mountains of statistics were accumulated by a subcommittee of the U.S.A. Senate in its "Survey of Profit-Sharing" (1938) to demonstrate that profit-sharing had been practiced successfully by large impersonal corporations as well as by small firms.

The objections of labor to profit-sharing, on the grounds that it is an uncertain form of reward and hampers organization, can be overcome. This was demonstrated in the experiment of a Birmingham (England) Rotarian who had had a long experience in sharing his profits. Some skeptics told him: "Yes, men will behave all right while it pays them. If circumstances were such that by showing goodwill it would affect their pockets, there would be a different tale to tell." Also, he heard some trade-unionists say that a firm that has profits to share should pay them out directly in higher wages.

The Rotarian was so impressed by this last argument that he decided to present such a scheme to his employees—an end to profit-sharing and a general raise in wages. To his surprise, the general meeting of employees received the plan without enthusiasm. Everyone agreed that it was quite generous, but each man who spoke seemed to have the fear that it would spoil the good spirit that had existed hitherto. One remarked that they had ceased to think of their jobs merely in terms of what they were going to get out of them, and did not want to be deprived of their dignity as *partners*.

A business that distributes half of its net profits to employees and is now five times as profitable as in the old days when the owner kept all the profits for himself, found that it could accomplish this happy result only with the co-operation of the union. Membership in the union was made a prerequisite of sharing. Dividends were paid monthly according to the changing ratio of the sales value of production to labor costs. With the co-operation of the union in allowing workers to change jobs and to help each other, unit efficiency increased 54 per cent in the first year.

But what of the non-profit organization? Where there is no opportunity for profit-sharing, or similar employee incentives, can other means be found to provide the square deal for employees?

Rotarians need only to look to their central office in Evanston and to its branch offices to find the answer to this question. Rotary International is strictly a non-profit organization. Its revenue is from a fixed per-capita contribution of its member clubs. Its income increases only in proportion to the increase in the size of the organization—and such increase brings with it a corresponding increase in expenses. Here is found a staff, averaging some 160 persons, who can have no delusion that increased production will result automatically in increased revenue, which will, in turn, be reflected in the pay envelope. They are not dealing with production units and follow no sales graphs or charts. They deal in intangibles. Their interest is in quality production rather than quantity.

Yet those Rotarians, who have worked closely with these men and women as members of the board of directors or of Rotary International committees, have never failed to marvel at the loyalty, the sincerity, and the *esprit de corps* of the staff.

Add to this the fact that the governing body of Rotary International undergoes an almost complete change of personnel annually and a complete change every two years and one wonders, therefore, what may be the secret of this spirit of co-operation between employer and employee. Frankly, there is no secret. It is merely an example of vocational service in action. Rotary International practices what it preaches. Rotary International provides for its employees pleasant working conditions and a healthful, friendly atmosphere in which to work.

Surely, the principles of vocational service are getting more than lip-service at the headquarters of Rotary International—and in the branches of that office. Rotarians are cordially invited to inspect these "plants" at the first opportunity.

In all these efforts that Rotarians and others are making to achieve a square deal with employees, the keynote is expansion, increased efficiency, and employee satisfaction. In the square deal, the employee plays his part, convinced and inspired by the good faith manifested by the employer. He begins to identify his interest with the firm and to share the vision of its possibilities. He comes to appreciate the role of capital

97

in storing up profits for a rainy day and investing in new machinery to improve the productivity of labor.

When the first census of manufacturers in the U.S.A. was taken 105 years ago, the average worker was putting in 69 hours a week and took home $4.74. The manufacturer had on the average $557 invested for each worker he employed. Today the employer has about $10,000 invested for each worker who puts in about half as many hours and draws nearly twenty times as many dollars. The importance of this form of profit-sharing will not be lost on the employee who appreciates a square deal, and he will seek to reciprocate by refraining from wildcat strikes, by meeting production standards, and by striving to attain the qualities of the faithful employee specified in the following statement:

A SEARCH FOR MEN

Wanted

A man for hard work and rapid promotion, a man who can find things to do without the help of a manager and three assistants.

A man who gets to work on time in the morning and does not imperil the lives of others in an effort to be the first out at night.

A man who is neat in appearance.

A man who does not sulk for an hour's overtime in emergencies.

A man who listens carefully when he is spoken to and asks only enough questions to insure the accurate carrying out of instructions.

A man who looks you straight in the eye and tells you the truth every time.

A man who does not pity himself for having to work.

APPLY ANYWHERE: The world is searching for such men.

A SQUARE DEAL FOR EMPLOYEES

Perhaps Winston Churchill was thinking of such men when he described his view of the square deal enlarged to a national scale:

"Our aim is to build a property-owning democracy, both independent and interdependent. In this I include profit-sharing schemes in suitable industries and intimate consultation between employers and wage-earners. We seek as far as possible to make the status of the wage-earner that of a partner rather than an irresponsible employee.

"It is in the interest of the wage-earner to have many other alternatives open to him than service under one all-powerful employer called the State. We do not wish the people of this ancient island reduced to a mass of State-directed proletarians, thrown hither and thither, housed here and there, by an aristocracy of privileged officials or trade-union bosses. Our ideal is a consenting union of free, independent families, and homes."

Perhaps the first step in realizing this ideal is for employers to subject their present arrangements in rewarding and advancing their employees to a careful scrutiny. They might ask themselves questions such as those suggested by a British Rotarian in writing on "Incentives":

(1) Are the people in production sure of receiving justice from all grades of management?

(2) Have they a sense of security?

(3) Is effort made to keep them fit?

(4) Do the wages they receive insure the security of decent living?

(5) Are they convinced that they will be promoted if they have the ability?

(6) Is the paramount incentive, creative activity aroused?

(7) Do they feel the sense of dignity of man in the work they perform?

(8) Are they made to feel the sense of duty, to get the spirit of their responsibility and their duty to the community?

(9) Do they realize that the dignity of man means the application of inescapable duties?

Even though it may not be practical to redeal the cards immediately, it should be possible to remove the suspicion that whim or accident is a controlling factor. To establish confidence in his own good intentions is essential for any employer who hopes to inspire goodwill and earnest effort.

*How do you plan to achieve
a square deal with your
employees?*

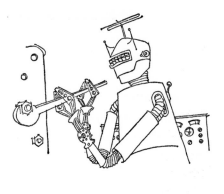

11

Robots or Human Beings

NEVER is the need for confidence in the good faith of employers more keenly tested than in periods of great change. The evil done in the early stages of the industrial revolution lived long after that generation of employers. Conditions of employment in mine and mill spelled appalling misery and degradation for the mass of workers. Joy in craftsmanship was exchanged for slavery to the machine. Cheap products found reflection in commercial practices equally debased. Only after a century of bitter struggle was it possible to restore in part the standards that had been sacrificed on the altar of mechanized progress.

Vocational service as it has developed in Rotary can be seen as one phase of the effort to repair the human and social damages inflicted by the Industrial Revolution. And who can say that the task is completed?

Even now, it is said, we are on the threshold of a Second Industrial Revolution. Whereas machines bound the worker to monotonous, repetitious jobs, new machines are emerging to replace him and to do those jobs better. Whereas the First Industrial Revolution substituted mechanical for muscular power, automation substitutes mechanical for human judgment, and mechanical judgment is infallible. Robots will undertake the robot functions that human beings have performed, and human beings will be freed to exercise higher skills.

"Automation, well used," a Belgian Rotarian told his club, "undertakes only what is not properly thought, but reflex. Therefore, we should rejoice in this economic progress which is also social progress."

Well used. The qualifying phrase is all important. No doubt the First Industrial Revolution when it was launched promised as much, had it been "well used." But the employers of that day were not conscious of the problems of transition. To them, the worker was just something for which a machine had not been invented: a robot. Has the present generation of employers a deeper understanding of the function of human beings in production that will enable them to surmount the problems of transition posed by automation—problems of upgrading and training employees for higher skills, of adjustment to new forms of competitive enterprise, and of distributing an accelerated production?

A British Rotarian writes:

"Nowhere can Rotarians make a more vital contribution in vocational service than by giving earnest and constant thought to this problem: How can I humanize my concern? How can I make every man, woman, boy, or girl who works for me realize that in a real sense they are my business family, sharing with me the toil, the ambitions, the achievements, the hopes, the sorrows, and the rewards of a joint adventure?"

On all sides, leaders in commerce and industry are pointing to human engineering as a new frontier. Said the heir to one great industrial empire, "If we can solve the problems of human relations in production, I believe we can make as much progress toward lower costs in the next ten years as we made during the past hundred through the development of the machinery of mass production."

These opinions were not conceived synthetically to beautify after-dinner orations. They were born under the compulsions of three shattering experiences, universal in their impact and of great practical consequence—the world depression, the world war, and the power struggle following the war. Each of these experiences demonstrated in different ways that the idea of "economic man" was too simple, that people could not be accurately defined as "something for which a machine had not been invented," that the su-

preme problem of this generation was to match progress in technology with progress in human relations.
To state the problem is not to solve it, however.
Human engineering has a long way to go before it
catches up with mechanical engineering, and when
business men contemplate this enterprise they may
well recall the lines of Santayana:

> Our knowledge is a torch of smoky pine
> That lights the pathway but one step ahead
> Across a void of mystery and dread.

Scientists are usually the last to dogmatize, for they
know how often their most cherished theories are over-
thrown. One investigation by Harvard professors de-
voted five years to observing the same girls doing the
same job. Every conceivable variation in their personal
lives and the conditions of their employment was carefully correlated with their output. Everyone was happy
with the results because improved working conditions
seemed to improve the output and the earnings of the
workers. But then one investigator proposed to restore
the original conditions—the forty-eight-hour week without rests, lunches, etc. Output, instead of declining as
expected, maintained its high level. The theory that
improved conditions and absence of fatigue automatically increased output seemed discredited.

A world-famous manufacturer of electrical equipment experimented with the effects of different lighting
on the productivity of workers. To control the experiment, a group of individuals with no discoverable personality problems was selected and every provision was
made for their contentment. With perfect lighting for
their work, production of this group soared. When

lighting was reduced it made no difference. Finally, working under an illumination no better than moonlight, this group remained as productive as ever. Evidently, workers who are satisfied can over come physical handicaps.

What are these powerful sentiments in human beings that underlie and often supersede the obvious incentives of improved conditions and rewards? That is a question that must interest not only employers, but salesmen, teachers, doctors, and dentists, in fact, anyone whose work calls for a deep-down understanding of people. Answers vary infinitely and gain by being specific, but here is a general conclusion reached by the Labor and Management Center of Yale University.

The goals of the human organism, whether it house a floor-sweeper or the president of a company, are to gain—

(1) The respect of his fellow-men;

(2) Material comforts and as much economic security as the most favored;

(3) Increasing control of his own affairs;

(4) Better understanding of forces and factors at work in his world;

(5) A basis of integrity for living.

This brief excursion along the frontier of human engineering may suggest the type of investigation that is taking place today. If it seems rather theoretical, Rotarians may recall the remark of Michael Faraday when he was showing his first experiment in electromagnetism. A member of parliament asked him of what use it was, and Faraday replied: "Well, of what use is a newborn baby? But you may be able to tax this some day."

Rather more might be claimed for human engineering as it is being developed, not only in the study of employees, but in all phases of vocational service. Each business or professional relationship that involves people calls for careful examination of their goals, their sentiments, and their abilities. It calls for constant re-evaluation of personal attitudes and policies in the light of this examination. Each store, each office, each workshop, each factory is a laboratory of human engineering where living, vital knowledge is waiting to be organized.

From this viewpoint, the "recognition of the worthiness of all useful occupations" enjoined by Rotary's Object, acquires an *active* significance. As eloquently described in a speech by the president of a Chinese Rotary club in the Far East, it involves humility, understanding, and leadership.

"The occupation of the cobbler," he declared, "with his little rap-atap-tap stand on the street corner or the shoe-shine boy yelling to you 'Shoe shine, Joe?' along the sidewalk is just as worthy and dignified as the occupation of any banker with his office luxuriously fitted with panelled walls, telephones, cushions, and swivel chairs and all the fineries becoming of his occupation. However humble an occupation be, it is up to the man to make it worthy and dignified.

"Have you ever had the experience of taking a rickshaw ride without previous bargaining as to the price of the ride? Then, at the end of the journey, you give the rickshaw-puller a certain sum of money and he voluntarily returns to you some change without your asking? Well I have had that experience. More than once. Now what do you think of that rickshaw-puller? In my opinion, that rickshaw-puller has high standards in his business of rickshaw-pulling. He recognizes the dignity of his occupation. He feels that in accepting the whole sum of money you give him for the ride, he would be charging you an exorbitant price for his work. Ostensibly, he is trying to be fair to you. But subconsciously, he is rendering a distinct service to the community.

"These men, though they are not Rotarians and though their occupations are about the most humble in the social scale, are exemplifying not only the principles of Rotary, but are building upon the real foundation of all successful business enterprise—'*business is service*'. What these humble non-Rotarians are able to accomplish in their efforts to serve society, we as Rotarians should be able to do better; yes, in comparing the advantages we have over these men of humble occupation, we should be able to do thousands of times better."

A confession comes from a Rotarian, so distinguished for his relations with his employees that he was selected as an employer-representative at the International Labor Conference. As the result of some unhappy experiences on the eve of his departure, he was feeling rather bitter about labor in general as he crossed the ocean. One evening in company with some fellow-delegates in the smoking-room, this feeling came to the surface in a somewhat vehement expression of misgivings concerning the whole picture of labor-management relations. In the midst of his lament, one of the delegates suddenly interrupted him. "Look here," he said, "I'm going to ask you a question. Don't think. Just answer right away—quick! *Do you like your men?*"

As the Rotarian tells the story, he was considerably taken aback. "Do you know, I was unable to answer that question right away. If he had asked me whether I loved my wife or children, I would have said 'yes' without thinking. But when he put that question up to me and I couldn't answer it, I knew there was something wrong with me. I should like to ask you— any of you—to go and sit down in a quiet corner and ask yourselves that question and see what your answer would be.

"The delegate's advice to me was, 'Go home and like them, and see the difference.' "

Employees are people. Like all people, they like to be liked. It makes a difference that can be apparent in many ways. The visitor to a large plant where some marvelous new machines had been installed, commented to the president of the company: "They certainly are beauties, and I expect they cost you a pretty penny. But they weren't what impressed me particularly. What struck me as we walked through those great shops was the look on the faces of your employees, the ready smile and the words exchanged with some of them. It showed that these people were glad to work with you and that even big business need not lose the personal touch."

Treating employees as people involves inevitably the consideration of matters only remotely connected with their jobs. Tangible demonstrations of this friendly concern with the physical, social, and spiritual well-being of employees are legion. Provision of comfortable and healthy working conditions carries over naturally to the furnishing of free medical care and hospitalization for the employee and his dependents, economical housing, recreational facilities, paid vacations, and pensions.

"We try to make our workers' lives worth living," was the simple explanation of one firm which had provided for the welfare of employees in *all* these ways.

Another firm which supported an exclusive country club for the recreation of its employees and their families proclaimed: "At the heart of our plan is the belief that the healthy worker will out-produce the sickly one, and that a happy worker will do more work and do it better, than a discontented one."

Nor are these efforts to treat employees like people confined to large and wealthy corporations. The small organization with its intimate first-name relationships can and often does plan extensively for its employees' welfare. A Canadian employer told his vocational craft assembly at a Rotary convention how "we organize our workmen."

"We have bowling leagues in the wintertime," he stated, "and we give a banquet for them at the end of the season. We have picnics for them in the summertime. We have hockey games. Many of them go fishing and they bring back pictures of their catch. We give a prize for the biggest fish caught. They get a great kick out of it. You have got to work for those fellows because they are working for you. Pay them back in something besides coin, because coin won't buy everything in this day and age."

In a pamphlet called "Firm Foundations" issued by the Rotary Club of Capetown, South Africa, small business is advised how it can help its employees through savings plans, group insurance, and the guarantee of loans. A medical-aid society in which firms with only a few employees can participate was launched in Rhodesia. And for those who may doubt Rotary's influence in vocational service, it should be noted that the impetus for this scheme came from the vocational service chairman of a Rotary club.

Employers who like their workers and think of them as people do not lack inspiring examples of tangible ways to express their sentiments. The list of benefits and welfare projects is inexhaustible and, in some ways, bewildering. Questions arise. Do employees appreciate what they are getting? Are these costly gratuities justified in terms of heightened morale, increased productivity, reduced labor turnover and less-frequent absences from work? Or are these typical replies taken from a recent poll of employees an indication that treating them like people may sometimes misfire?

"I thought the government paid for it."

"They take it out of our pay."

"I didn't even know there were such benefits."

"It's paternalism!"

Such comments are not at all uncommon. As a response to a friendly gesture they are sometimes hard to take. Yet they do illustrate the dangers inherent in all social undertakings. That enlightened despot of Prussia who carried his concern for his subjects' welfare so far that he went around dipping his finger into their cooking pots to assure himself that they were getting the right nourishment, is a warning to all of us. The self-conscious philanthropist with "an over-powering air of doing good" is generally resented and often suspected.

The mistakes of paternalism and all its disappoint-ments can be avoided if common sense is mixed in liberal quantities with sentiment. A frank and objec-tive recognition that the money spent on these bene-fits could be added to the workers' pay may lead to the decision that they should be consulted about the proj-ect being planned. Or the individual employee can be left completely free to decide without stigma to his reputation as a "good fellow" whether he wants to participate in activities sponsored by the firm. In this way the concept that "employees are people" can be stretched to include the realization that they are "per-sons" too, with freedom of choice, and therefore more likely to join in where they have complete liberty to refuse.

On the other hand, enlightened self-interest should never be masked under a spurious benevolence. Gen-eral statistics show that absenteeism costs as much as the average company's net profit. Labor turnover in many plants runs as high as 50 per cent a year; and the cost of recruitment, placement, and training, even of an unskilled worker, averages close to a hundred dol-lars. Accordingly, there is ample justification of ex-penditures that help to keep employees healthy in mind and body, free from worry and happy in their jobs. The benefits that produce these results can often be made available to employees as a group far more economically than they could be obtained individually.

Frank explanation of these facts to employees can help remove any suspicion of paternalism.

Robots or human beings? In the last analysis, is it not a question of self-esteem? Happy is the worker who prides himself in the importance of his function. A Rotarian happened to sit next to a passenger on the bus who seemed completely wrapped up in his own thoughts. Every so often a smile flitted across his face.

"You seem to be enjoying this ride, friend," the Rotarian ventured to remark. The man started; then relaxed and smiled. "I must have looked silly," he said, "but I have a good reason. I was just checking up on my engine."

"What do you mean, *your* engine?" came back the Rotarian. "I though it belonged to the Blank Bus Company."

"Oh, sure," he answered, "but it's still my baby. I've just put in two solid days on that power plant, and now listen to her, will you. Purring like a contented cat. Look," he went on, "I hammer and measure and grind and adjust these motors for months at a time, and when I send them out on the road, they're right! But the greatest enjoyment I get is when I sit here with thirty other passengers and see how the bus performs. It gives me a lift," said he, "when I remember that the work I do in the shop is safety insurance for hundreds of people who ride these buses."

In what ways can a Rotarian
employer help to revive
the spirit of craftsmanship?

12

Industry's Future Manpower

WHAT an amazing world this would be if everyone could be convinced suddenly that *service is my business.* The discontents and the discord would melt away. The mountainous problems that hamper production and distribution would become soluble. Teamwork would replace suspicion and frustration. Imagine a factory, an office, or a retail store where everyone *lived* vocational service, spontaneously and without affectation, as a natural way of living. What a pleasure to be associated in any way, as a competitor or a customer, with such an institution!

Rotarians who consider seriously the possibility of helping to realize this dream are well aware of the difficulties. They recognize them as they exist in their own personalities and in those with whom they seek to co-operate. Selfishness—prejudice—fear—are built into so many of us by harsh experience, perhaps, or by early training. However we got that way, it makes it very difficult for us to live consistently as if service *were* our business.

But, if we really want to realize this dream, it would seem that the most hopeful subject would be the new generation of workers just entering upon their careers. To these youngsters, the idea that *service is my business* will hold intriguing possibilities. Beneath any protective veneer of cheap cynicism he or she may have accumulated, youth is idealistic. As they enter business life the will to believe is strong, hopes are high. What an opportunity to serve society has the employer of these young hopefuls—an opportunity that can be seized energetically, but too often is woefully ignored.

The program planning committee of Rotary International has recommended that the following statement be brought to the attention of all Rotarians who are employers of youth.

INDUSTRY'S FUTURE MANPOWER

1. That every Rotarian engaged in industry and who is the employer of adolescent young persons and/or engages the services of youth direct from school, should constitute himself the friend and advisor, especially during working hours, of each such person in his employ, whether it be in the workshop, factory, or office.

2. It is suggested that he should, to this end, interview personally each young person being considered for employment or already employed and explain:

(a) The difference between work as a means of earning a living and work as a way of living a life;

(b) The importance to himself and to the community of the new phase of life into which the youth has entered;

(c) The fact that real and practical education and learning begins and does not end upon leaving school;

(d) That the acquiring of further academic and scientific knowledge is an essential addition to vocational activities and skill in order to be a success in life and vocation;

(e) That immense satisfaction and happiness are attainable from the effort to improve one's knowledge and education and that such effort, when added to good conduct and character, rarely fails to produce material as well as spiritual well-being;

(f) That the Rotarian employer is personally interested in him or her and may be regarded as a real friend and advisor.

3. That each Rotarian employer of youth should take an active interest in the physical welfare of those employes, encouraging them to join physical-fitness classes, etc.

4. That each Rotarian employer of youth (especially of school-leavers) should encourage such young persons to take advantage of the facilities available in almost every town and city for continued education in day school or at evening classes.

5. That the Rotarian should make a special point of seeing that such youth, upon joining his firm or company, are placed under the charge of foremen or directive employees who will and can guide them in the acquisition of good habits and manner of work leading to the development of skill and interest in their work.

6. That the Rotarian's personal interest in the youth be expressed, if possible, to their parents and the utmost encouragement and co-operation of the latter be sought.

Many Rotarians are attempting to apply these suggestions methodically in their own enterprises, just as many Roary clubs are organizing occupational information by their members for youth who are choosing a career. By a recent decision of the board of directors of Rotary International, these club projects are considered as vocational service—*if* the information includes definite explanations of the concept of service in each occupation.

The employer who says to himself, "Service is my business," and really believes it, will interest himself in the youth he employs and in more ways than any set of recommendations can outline. He will regard these young people, not as mere means of production, but as ends in themselves, as constituting a part at least of the purpose of his business. His business may be the building of great cranes to lift the burdens of humanity, but just as surely he is also building lives. Future generations will witness how well he has builded.

*Are you developing cordial, helpful
relations with the younger
employees in your business?*

116

13

A Basis for Agreement

ONCE, it is told, the workers of ancient Rome arose and went on strike. Declaring that they would no longer toil for their masters, they withdrew to a nearby hill. Rome was paralyzed, and the patricians waited apprehensively as Menenius Agrippa went to persuade the strikers to return. He told them this fable: "The members of the human body once mutinied against the belly and accused it of lying idle and useless while they were all laboring and toiling to satisfy its appetites. But the belly only laughed at the simplicity of those who knew not that though it received all the nourishment into itself, it prepared and distributed it again to all parts of the body."

Just so, said Agrippa, stands the case between the employers and the strikers. He won his case. But the argument has continued to this day. Millions of man-days of production and billions in wages are lost through strikes. Incalculable injury is suffered by others. Shortages and rising prices caused by strikes stoke the fires of inflation and add to the threat of depression and dictatorship.

Yet, the real nature of the crisis in labor relations is not revealed by detailing its disastrous consequences. Strikes are like a thermometer which indicates that the boiling-point has been reached. They disclose the situation. They are not the situation itself. Just as you cannot reduce the temperature of a room by applying an ice-bag to the thermometer, so making strikes difficult will not relieve the tensions of industry. You have to get the temperature down by finding the cause of the excessive heat and removing it.

Surely Rotary should have some answer to the problem of labor conflict. The interest of its members as business and professional men is involved. Their influence is not inconsiderable. The deeper relation of the crisis to the personal attitudes of workers and employers challenges their professed ideals.

It may be helpful at the outset to dispose of the defeatist notion that the conflict is inevitable. This notion stems directly from the interpretation of history as a class struggle proposed by Karl Marx, though it is often shared by people very far from being Marxists. Whoever assumes that workers are concerned only with getting the most pay for the least work or that employers have no other thought but profit, con-

118

sciously or unconsciously, subscribes to the doctrine of Marxian materialism. On this basis alone does conflict between them seem irreconcilable.

Nor is the idea of inevitable conflict any longer supported by the modern biologist who has abandoned the Darwinian description of "nature, red in tooth and claw" in favor of one that attributes the survival of species to co-operation. "Co-operate or die" is the law of life, according to Professor Allee writing on Animal Sociology in the *Encyclopedia Britannica*.

Discredited theories die hard. There is a time-lag before they are abandoned. Repudiated in principle, the theory of the class struggle often survives in practice and crops out in the strangest places. How many employers, for instance, approach the bargaining table as rigidly determined to battle for their class rights as the most impassioned agitator. The single thought of both parties to the dispute is the desire to *dominate*.

The desire to dominate lies at the very heart of the system that produces strikes. Where each party is out to win, to impose his will upon the other, to prescribe his own solution whatever discouragement or frustration it may cause—conflict is indeed inevitable. Even if the weakness of one party prevents open strife, a sullen spirit of resentment sours the relationship. The co-operation essential to survival becomes impossible. What degree of efficiency or initiative or loyalty could an employer expect who dominated his employees without regard to their welfare or respect for their rights?

Domination rarely succeeds in any kind of a situation. In a labor dispute, the result is usually a *com-*

promise. Each side renounces a part of its aim to dominate when the struggle has become too painful. This kind of solution is often hailed as a victory for moderation, and such it may be. But too often it represents merely reluctant concession and appeasement in the worst sense. Its consequences may be no less disastrous than the choice of the man cycling home after dark along a country road. He saw two lights coming toward him. "Sure, and I'll steer between them," he said. Unfortunately they were the lights of a truck. Too often a compromise merely confirms the will to dominate eventually. It encourages stubbornnesses and insincerity. The sterile issue of much haggling, it leaves both combatants with the feeling that they have been beaten and with the determination to renew the struggle when they have gathered new strength.

Obsessed by the conviction that conflict is inevitable, employers and employees and their representatives ignore completely the possibility of an alternative procedure to one based on the desire to dominate and ending in compromise. Yet a definite and distinct alternative does exist, and with it the chance for leadership out of the barren wilderness of labor strife.

The key word is *combination.* It describes a procedure which seeks to absorb the conflicting interests in an overriding common interest.

One such common interest might be simply a mutual recognition that conflict is costly and sterile. Everyone loses in a strike. Or it might be the common fear of both parties that their conflict would lead to government controls and bureaucratic interference equally distasteful to employers and unions. These negative

120

interests, however, do not point to any particular solution. They do not release the energies which conflict diverts from the useful side of life. A common interest that was positive, rather than negative, would have greater creative force.

A British industrialist, Sir George Schuster, formulated such a positive basis for agreement when he told the London Rotary Club that "the goal of both labor and management should be to increase the size of the cake rather than quarrel over how it should be divided." Increased individual productivity, lower prices, and expanded sales were the positive goals that he suggested.

Still more comprehensive as a basis for agreement is the formula expressed in the concluding words of the second phase of Rotary's Object—*"service to society."* Translated into practical and specific proposals for any given business or industry, these words are revolutionary in their import. They suggest that instead of basing their demands on near-sighted selfish considerations, labor—and management, too—should relate them to a common interest in expanding business, higher living standards, and general prosperity.

Would the intractable problems, the sullen discontents, the accumulated bitterness that have encompassed labor conflict, yield to such an approach? Could tough-minded, horse-trading negotiators be persuaded to try it instead of retracing with hopeless doggedness the dreary paths of domination and compromise? How much persuasive skill would be required to convince cynical or obdurate minds that this inspirational phrase

—"service to society"—offers real hope, not merely for preventing strikes but for impairing a new spirit of real co-operation? There is no foretelling until the attempt has been made.

Rotarians who decide to make the experiment, whether in a store with half a dozen employees or in a factory with several hundred, whether in negotiation with previously estranged labor leaders or in conversation with the new girl at the notion counter—will be aware that they are attempting something of great significance.

Each problem will invoke a different style of approach. But in every case, three steps are essential:

(1) The basis of agreement—"service to society"—must be explained and perhaps rephrased to convey all its implications in concrete, tangible terms so that the individual employee or labor representative will see clearly his relation to it. At the same time, the Rotarian will frankly set forth what he conceives to be his own relation to this common interest.

(2) The special interests of both parties must be considered in the light of the common interest. All the cards must be laid on the table. There should be no shrinking from the fighting words, the belligerently expressed demands, nor suppression of any accumulated grievances and mistrust. But once these have been stated, both parties should try to re-evaluate them in terms of "service to society."

This critical step in the procedure calls for a little elaboration. The aim is to find out what each party really wants, and to see how these private goals can be reconciled with the common goal. Suppose, for instance, a dispute in which the workers demanding increased take-home pay are met with the objection that the employer has to make a profit in a competitive market. Break down this demand and this objection in terms of what each party really wants. Translate those real wants in terms of "service to society." Compare them. Could they not be reconciled? Combined? Almost identified?

THE EMPLOYEES REALLY WANT—
A fair day's pay
Security
Real incentives
Recognition
A share in policy-making

THE EMPLOYER REALLY WANTS—
A fair day's work
Loyalty and goodwill
Increased productivity
Initiative and ideas
A fair return on investment

Are not these the real wants that underlie the haggling over wages and hours, welfare funds, vacations with pay, and a thousand other issues? Are they not quite reasonable and honest desires that can be *satisfied*—not compromised—through a common agreement of service to society?

(3) The procedure is not complete without action. Agreement on a common goal, the most satisfying talk, will only end in disillusionment if tangible

results do not follow quickly. The extent of the action is dependent on many circumstances, but its nature should be such as to reveal plainly the reconciliation of the separate interests of the parties to the agreement. Immediate action—looking forward to continued action—is an earnest of good faith.

Rotarians who undertake these three steps as an alternative to the procedure of domination and compromise can expect results only over a period. This application of Rotary is a slow process. It extends far beyond the immediate crisis produced by strikes until it embraces all employer-employee relations.

What specific contributions Rotarians and Rotary clubs can make to develop this much-needed understanding is something for individual determination. That the spirit of "service to society" is already at home in the labor relations of many Rotarians is apparent. Yet the idea could be expressed more openly and directly. Even in the smallest business it could become the theme for discussion at meetings with employees. Even professional men could give currency to the idea by frankly presenting it to competitors, colleagues, or clients as a basis for agreement. Through education, influence, and example, the opportunity existing everywhere for "combined operations" could provide a powerful antitoxin to the prevailing class conflict.

A special opportunity exists in relation to trade-union leaders. Like the men whose vocation is management, these professional trade-unionists are sensitive to any threat against their own particular status and prerogative. There is nothing discreditable in this. It is perfectly natural. When labor leaders express a zeal to share in managerial functions, when management through interest in human engineering seeks ways to win greater efficiency, the other party is likely to exclaim: "Production? Service? Yes, but not over *my* dead body!"

Anyone who feels professionally insecure is likely to look around for ways to stress the importance of his function. The employer does this, sometimes, by means of distance and secrecy. Let no one penetrate the "holy of holies" where he is mystically managing to meet the payroll on Saturday night. The trade-union executive, on the other hand, may feel impelled to justify his position by assuming the role of an Oliver Twist. His prerogatives will be respected by dues-paying members so long as he is continually "asking for more." No sooner has he negotiated one set of labor gains than he begins to hint about the next series of demands. How else is he to justify his existence?

Would it not contribute enormously to the professional security of the trade-union executive if a Rotarian employer would invite him to general consultation on their respective roles as seen in the light of "service to society"? In the course of consultation, the opportunity for combined operations between them could be explored. As partners, rather than rivals, each could benefit. Or a Rotary club at one of its meetings could present a trade-union leader with the same question, and work out with him a program for expanding this project throughout the labor movement. Or the same club might consider the possibility of filling the classification officially described as "Labor Organizations" with an intelligent and statesmanlike representative who would make it *his* business to promote combined operations.

Who can tell what may be the wide repercussions from such contacts. Eight years ago, the vocational service committee in Auckland, New Zealand invited two trade unionists to attend its meeting. They came hesitatingly, but enjoyed the discussion and brought several of their colleagues to subsequent meetings. The upshot was the formation of a labor-management group which prepared a joint statement of principles similar to those which have been considered here.

In 1951, a very serious situation arose on the waterfront of Auckland. A strike threatened to become an attempt to overthrow constitutional government. Police measures could not deal with the disorders, but the attempt failed because responsible union leaders, many of them members of this group inspired by Rotary, were able to convince the rank and file of the employer's sincerity. It was their own conviction obtained through personal acquaintance and experience.

Has your club considered the possibility of inviting a trade unionist to become a member?

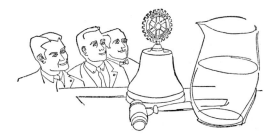

14

Operation Rotary Club

A T the beginning of this book, vocational service was defined as an obligation of each member of a Rotary club to SHARE the ideal of Rotary with non-Rotarians he meets or contacts in his business or profession. Viewed in this light, the opportunities for practical, down to earth activities in vocational service are legion. Many of the ways in which the individual Rotarian is challenged to share Rotary in his own business and professional life have already been illustrated. It remains to suggest the scope for club and committee work.

Recommendations by the program planning commitee of Rotary International for the observance of the Golden Anniversary in 1955 contained no less than fifty specific and distinct activities for clubs to undertake in vocational service. These by no means exhaust the possibilities. The experience and procedures of many successful vocational service projects are available on request from the secretariat of Rotary International, 1600 Ridge Avenue, Evanston, Illinois, U.S.A. With these resources, any club anywhere can expect its vocational service committee to develop a thorough plan that will stimulate each and every member to fulfill his obligation of sharing Rotary in his business or profession.

The club meeting is a natural setting for this plan. Programs by the vocational service chairmen responsible for employee, competitor, buyer-seller, trade associations, and Four-Way Test* activities can point out to members their opportunities for sharing in these fields. The "classification talk" traditional in Rotary only fulfills its purpose if the member making it explains just how he is making the influence of Rotary felt in his business or profession. Sometimes that purpose is achieved by having the talk made by a fellow member who has made an investigation of his practices. Several short dramatizations of vocational service problems are available to spark discussion at the club meeting.

Experience proves, however, that coming to grips with these problems requires more time than the program at the club meeting affords. The leisurely and informal gathering of a small group in the home of a member is better for exchanging ideas about actual situations and for formulating plans of action. Some two hundred vocational service committees in the British Isles, for instance, have been studying how Rotary

*See page 137.

can help to increase productivity in factory and office. An alternative supplement to the club program is the club forum on vocatonal service. Typical was the experience of a district governor in Argentina who designated host clubs and leaders, issued invitations and outlined topics for discussion. A number of these forums were so successful that their practical results were recorded in a widely distributed pamphlet.

Another stimulating experience developed sometimes on the district level or by groups of clubs is the Rotary Business Relations Conference. Leaders in different fields of vocational service interest give expert advice, both publicly and privately, to large gatherings of Rotarians. So valuable have these conferences proved that one district has continued to hold them for fifteen years. Three such conferences dealing particularly with the situation of the aging worker were presented by another district governor.

So far the types of sharing considered have been the kind that inform and stimulate Rotarians to action in their individual business and professional lives. The Rotary club can also provide direct assistance to such actions. This book and The Four-Way Test are tools for sharing the concept that "service is my business" with non-Rotarians in all the relationships of business or profession. They provide bridges that the Rotarian can use in communicating to employees, competitors, customers or suppliers his desire for a new understanding and the standards by which he would like all transactions to be measured. Translated in many languages, The Four-Way Test is available in several styles for distribution. Small folders telling its story can be circularized to customers. Posters proclaim it as the measurment "of the things we think, say or do" in office or mill. Desk plaques remind executives or professional men to govern each decision by what they know in their own hearts is right.

Some clubs make a survey of the vocational service activities and problems of their members by means of a questionnaire. A vocational service clinic is then established to extend in new directions the practices which local experience has approved. A great number of club meetings are designated as competitor and employee days to help members improve these relationships. One club in Australia holds an annual picnic for members, employees and their families. Reminiscent of the practice which gave Rotary its name are visits by clubs to the plants, stores or offices of members. A vivid impression of Rotary can be given to employees of these concerns on such "Rotation Days."

Still another sphere of operation for the Rotary club and its vocational service committee is the sharing of the Rotary ideal with the community at large. There is no home town so blessed that its people cannot be inspired to better living by the vision of "service is my business." It may be that a labor-management group or a courtesy contest as described earlier would fill a need. Or perhaps the sights of local salespeople could be raised by the sponsoring of a school for salesmanship. To dramatize the worthiness of all useful occupations, Rotary clubs in Japan and elsewhere have featured periodic tributes to postal employees, telephone operators and street-cleaners. Wider public understanding of

Rotary aims in business and profession can be developed by a town-meeting or a discussion by members over the radio or television.

"Service," as has been said, "is always a contribution to the future." There is no more universal opportunity for vocational service than the early training of youth, the new generation of employees and leaders, to habits of right thinking and doing. What more glorious accomplishment could any vocational service committee hope to achieve than a thorough job of persuading the young people of their town to use The Four-Way Test?

A survey of vocational service around the world shows it assuming a variety of forms adapted to local needs. In one country, Rotarians may be found combatting the black market with personal approaches to leading dealers requesting them to display prices and price-lists. Here, the Rotary club organized an exhibit of thirty-five local industries. There, a code of practices is drawn up and adopted by local merchants or the vocational service committee is instrumental in bringing about an amicable settlement of labor trouble in local factories.

Important is the reference of vocational service projects to an actual need of the local situation. Equally important is the keenness of the local Rotarians who recognize the need and their own obligation to do something about it. In every club that deserves the name of Rotary, there must be some members prepared to take this initiative, for without vocational service in active operation Rotary has lost its meaning and mission. It may be the chairman of the vocational service committee whose enthusiasm provides the spark, or it may be someone else.

Just how this happens is illustrated in the account of one committee meeting in South Africa. "The discussion had drifted into abstract generalities," the chairman recalled, "when a member burst forth with the demand that we get down to cases. He then proceeded to outline an actual problem that he was facing in his own business. Here in the friendly atmosphere of Rotary was a man ready to open his heart, to put all his cards on the table, and to seek advice and counsel from his friends. In a flash, the committee saw the meaning of vocational service. The exchange of experiences that followed sounded the keynote for a year's program."

Perhaps the consideration of "Service is My Business" by a group in your club would provoke this entanglement of Rotary aspirations with the reality of conditions in your town. One thing suggests another. The actual experiences recorded here may not exactly duplicate your experience, but they may bring to mind the opportunities for sharing Rotary that exist in your town as they do everywhere.

Which project in vocational service
would prompt members of your club
to put Rotary to
work where they
work?

15

It's Your Move Now

How often the player at chess or checkers, as the game reaches its final stages receives the brusque reminder: "It's your move now!" That player might well be compared with the reader of this book. Here, too, many pieces have been moved about the board. Vocational service has been "played" in terms of craftsmanship, good faith, human engineering — in their many aspects. As in chess or checkers, some of the pieces may have been lost. The reader, like the player, has not retained them for his use. Yet some remain, and he is confronted with the question, what shall he do with them. "It's *your* move now!"

Similarly, a Rotarian impressed by the horizons of

opportunity to serve society is not unlike the player who speculates about some brilliant strategy for winning the game. He, too, is challenged to do something about it. The large contributions that vocational service can make to the world will not be accomplished through discussion, still less by solemn resolutions in Rotary clubs. The genius of Rotary is individual action. The product of Rotary is men. Particularly is this the case in vocational service. When a Rotarian, convinced of the challenge to leadership in business or profession asks impatiently, "Why doesn't someone *do* something about it?" he is promptly invited to—"look in the mirror, and meet someone who can and should."

What process is it that goes on inside a man when the discussion of ideal goals is translated into practical activity? Some light on this abstruse problem may be found in an episode that occurred in a steamship office where several applicants for the post of radio operator had gathered to be interviewed. Their excited discussion of the prospects for employment made them oblivious to the dots and dashes that began coming over the loud speaker.

About that time, another man entered the office and sat down quietly by himself. Suddenly he snapped to attention, walked into the private office, and in a few minutes came out smiling.

"Say," called out one of the group, "how did you get in ahead of us? We were here first."

"One of you would have got the job," the man replied, "if you had listened to the message from the loud speaker."

"What message?" they asked in surprise.

"Why, the code," he told them. "It said, 'The man I need must always be on the alert. The man who gets this message and comes directly into my private office will be placed in one of my ships as a radio operator.'"

How many Rotarians have listened to talks on vocational service at conventions, district meetings, or in their own clubs? How many have been alert to recognize the message that would send them back to their offices with a plan of action? There is no way of telling, and if it could be told, the record might not be very encouraging. The transition from thought to action is often devious and fraught with peril for the idea. So much depends on the disposition of the man himself, his methods and habits in dealing with ideas.

Accordingly, the Rotarian who has given some thought to vocational service may also recognize the need *to service himself vocationally.*

The specific application of vocational service to a particular business or professional practice may not be apparent immediately. On the surface, established routines may seem well enough, or the prospect of injecting an entirely fresh note into the complex interrelationships of an active organization may appear bewildering. The Rotarian who asks himself, "Where shall I start?" may find himself answering rather in the vein of the farmer who encountered a stranger hopelessly lost in the country.

"Which road do I take for Cincinnati?" inquired the traveller.

The farmer deliberated for awhile, and then in a

burst of confidence, "You know, if I were going to Cincinnati, I wouldn't start from here."

Yet, right here in the Rotarian's own office, store, or factory is the opportunity to serve society. Where should he begin? What particular phase of his many relationships most urgently requires attention?

One way to find out is in the series of questions called "A Vocational Service Score Card," a personal check-up sheet that is available from Rotary International. So phrased that they call for definite answers, these questions will demonstrate to anyone just where his vocational service has been lacking, if he will consider them in all honesty and sincerity. One prominent Rotarian who had checked himself with the score card confessed that after he had totalled his score he tore the paper into tiny pieces and threw them into the wastebasket hoping that the charwoman was not an addict of the "jig-saw" puzzle.

Most Rotarians who use the score card will find the need for improvement in some one phase of their vocational service emphasized in their answers. *There* is the place to begin!

The process of servicing himself vocationally cannot stop here, however. Business and professional practice goes on continuously from day to day, bringing new problems into focus, calling for practical decisions of greater or less importance. To realize, even with a shock, the need for improvement is not enough. An habitual attitude, proof alike against monotony and against surprise, must be developed.

Many Rotarians habitually set apart a few minutes

at the beginning of each day as *a quiet time* for previewing the day's work as an opportunity for service. They ask themselves: "What is being done in my business that ought *not* to be done?" "What things ought we to be doing that we are not doing?" They anticipate the decisions that they or their associates may be called upon to make, and try to judge them objectively in the light of social usefulness.

A simple standard of judgment that can be applied spontaneously to every contingency as it arises, is "The Four-Way Test of the things we think, we say or do."*

1. Is it the *TRUTH?*
2. It is *FAIR* to all concerned?
3. Will it build *GOODWILL* and *BETTER FRIEND-SHIPS?*
4. Will it be *BENEFICIAL* to all concerned?

The Rotarian who originated The Four-Way Test took over a large business that was on the rocks. An official of the bank which had given this company a large loan in its prosperous days, and expected to lose it, declared that he had never heard of a concern "so broke" coming back. Yet, by putting the "Test" in control of its policies, the business was piloted to solvency. Immediate sacrifice of profits that failed to square with these requirements was amply repaid by a more efficient organization, employee dependability, and the confidence of customers.

Let no one suppose that translating vocational service principles into practice can be achieved overnight. Said the originator of The Four-Way Test: "Though

---

*Copyright 1946, Rotary International.

we ask our stockholders, employees, distributors, and customers to let us know when we don't live up to the Test, after many years of sincere endeavor we feel that we are living up to about seventy per cent of our ideals. We regret that we haven't done better. Yet I can see that we are making progress in learning what The Four-Way Test really means."

Servicing himself vocationally extends beyond the "quiet time" when the Rotarian considers his business or professional problems in the light of social useful-ness. "Sharing" is no less essential, not only as insur-ance that the new directions will be carried out intelli-gently by associates, but also as a check on the resolu-tion and sincerity of the Rotarian himself. Talking them over with others subjects intentions that have been conceived in a moment of enthusiasm to some sort of check and challenge. The Rotarian who takes a framed copy of The Four-Way Test and hangs it in his office for all to see issues a tacit invitation to every cus-tomer and client to measure performance with profes-sions. Employees are given to understand what they can expect from their employer as well as what he expects of them. Even competitors are summoned to help in keeping the business "on the beam." Can any-one with experience in business or profession fail to see that such courageous sharing is sound from every standpoint? As one Rotarian remarked: "Here are all the tools to do a good and practical job in human relations."

Will you give these tools a fair trial, a thoughtful and thorough application to the problems and opportunities of your working day? To impart a new tone to your business or professional relationships may call for some courage and persistence. As a Rotary bulletin put it: "We must have the freedom to fail. Ford forgot to put a reverse gear in his first automobile. Edison once spent two million dollars on an invention that proved of little value. The galleries are full of critics. They play no ball. They fight no fights. They make no mistakes because they attempt nothing. Down in the arena are the doers. They make some mistakes because they attempt many things."

This is the mood of high adventure in which a Rotarian who has really caught the spirit of Rotary will regard his vocation. Many things are to be attempted in sharing with others his realization that "service is my business." The chance of occasional failures will not deter him for he knows that true success in his business or profession lies in making the attempt. For this cause came he into the world.

It's *your* move now! Whether a Rotarian score himself, has a daily "quiet time," or shares with his business associates his resolution to serve society; whatever means he may use for translating the ideas of vocational service into action and habit are strictly his own business. Somehow that transition must be made, however, if Rotary is to escape the charge that vocational service is theoretical, mystical, and intangible. Words, glittering generalities, persuasive examples, eloquent speeches will avail nothing unless Rotarians apply them. Vocational service will exist only as a spectre at the feast if it is not put to practical use.

The Spanish philosopher, Unamuno, tells of the aqueduct in Segovia. Built by the Romans 1800 years ago, it carried cool waters from the mountains to the thirsty city. Nearly sixty generations of men drank from it. Then came another generation which said: "This aqueduct is so great a marvel, it should be preserved for our children's children. We will relieve it of its centuries-old labors."

To give it well-earned rest, they introduced a modern water supply. Then it began to fall apart. Built as it had been from rough-hewn granite blocks without lime or cement, the sediment of centuries had formed a natural mortar. Now the dry sun made it crumble. What centuries could not destroy, idleness disintegrated.

And so it is with vocational service in Rotary. Respected, but unused and set apart from the active business life of Rotarians, it becomes misty and impractical. It tends to fall apart. Tried and tested in daily combat with the tough problems of business or professional practice, vocational service grows with fresh vitality and meaning. Like the ripples from a stone flung into a pool, the influence of Rotary can stir the stagnant waters of commerce. The lines run out in countless directions when the individual Rotarian uses vocational service in his business or profession. Today it can begin. It's *your* move now!

THE FOUR-WAY TEST

of the things we think, say or do

1   Is it the *TRUTH?*

2   Is it *FAIR* to all concerned?

3   Will it build *GOODWILL* and *BETTER FRIENDSHIPS?*

4   Will it be *BENEFICIAL* to all concerned?

PRINTED IN U.S.A.